U.S. Regional Deterrence Strategies

Kenneth Watman, Dean Wilkening
with John Arquilla, Brian Nichiporuk

W0115740

Prepared for the
United States Army and the
United States Air Force

Arroyo Center

Project AIR FORCE

RAND

With the Cold War over, U.S. national security strategy has shifted away from its focus on the former Soviet Union and toward possible U.S. regional involvements. As a consequence, the applicability to regional adversaries of virtually all the fundamental elements of U.S. strategy—which were developed during the Cold War with the Soviet Union—must be reevaluated. Among these fundamentals is the role of deterrence. Deterrence was the heart of U.S. strategy for countering the Soviets, both because the United States believed the Soviets were deterrable and because war with the Soviets was unacceptably dangerous. Much of what is called "deterrence theory" was developed specifically for this function. Therefore, regional strategy requires revisiting basic questions about deterrence. Should the United States base its regional strategy on deterrence? Can regional adversaries be deterred and, if so, by what? What resources can and should the United States devote to that objective?

This report represents an attempt to come to grips with these fundamental questions. As such, it should be of interest to policymakers, strategists, and military planners interested in the conceptual requirements for effective deterrence, as well as the operational and force structure implications that emerge should the United States make regional deterrence one of the pillars of its national military strategy. As an application of these concepts, a companion report[1] addresses the specific question of strategies for deterring nuclear

---

[1]Dean Wilkening and Kenneth Watman, *Nuclear Deterrence in a Regional Context*, Santa Monica, Calif.: RAND, MR-500-A/AF, 1994.

attacks against the United States or U.S. allies by regional nuclear powers. This second report should be of interest to policymakers interested in U.S. counterproliferation policy.

This research was conducted jointly under the Strategy, Doctrine, and Force Structure program of Project AIR FORCE and under the Strategy and Doctrine program of the Army Research Division's Arroyo Center. Project AIR FORCE and the Arroyo Center are two of RAND's federally funded research and development centers.

CONTENTS

FIGURES

TABLE

This report assesses the requirements of a deterrence strategy for application to potential regional adversaries. In particular, this report elucidates the character and motivations of potential regional adversaries that may make them more difficult to deter than the former Soviet Union, the circumstances under which U.S. deterrent threats will appear credible, and finally the general military requirements that, historically, have correlated with deterrence success.

CHARACTER AND MOTIVATIONS OF REGIONAL ADVERSARIES

Few states or leaders appear to be truly "crazy" or undeterrable. A more useful characterization of the motivations of potential adversaries is based not on "craziness" but rather on the critical distinction between adversaries motivated to gain and adversaries motivated to avert loss (where loss or gain is determined from the adversary's perspective). This distinction is crucial. States (as well as individuals) motivated to avert a loss in their status quo tend to take higher risks, particularly if that status quo is already marginal. States seeking gain, especially if they enjoy an already acceptable status quo, appear to be much less willing to take risks. It follows that leaders who are willing to take greater risks will be more difficult to deter, all else being equal. The Japanese attack on Pearl Harbor is a classic example of the risks leaders are willing to take to avert a deteriorating status quo, in this case hastened by the U.S. embargo on strategic materials.

What losses motivate leaders to take risks? An external threat to a state's survival is an obvious loss leaders seek to avert. However, for many regional states, another threat frequently arises—one that Western political analysts often overlook—namely, domestic political threats to the regime's survival. Many regional states live with chronic internal political instability arising out of the fragile character of their political systems. The leaderships of such states often enter into international crises in an effort to ameliorate their domestic problems. Put another way, the threatened loss these regimes are trying to avert is loss of their hold on power. As a result, their stakes are very high, and their risk-taking propensities are frequently much greater than others appreciate.

This dichotomy between states motivated by gain as opposed to averting loss has important implications for regional deterrence. States that are satisfied with their status quo, e.g., the former Soviet Union during the Cold War, should be relatively easy to deter, because they will likely be risk-averse decisionmakers. Moderately credible U.S. deterrent threats to deny the adversary a cheap victory should be sufficient. On the other hand, regional adversaries motivated to avert domestic political loses are usually willing to take high risks. For these cases, deterrence will require credible (from the adversary's perspective) U.S. threats to deny the adversary's objectives, perhaps with additional threats to punish the regime. Thus, the military problem of regional deterrence in this instance boils down to two factors: (1) ways in which the United States can make its deterrent threats credible and (2) military capabilities required for credible denial and punishment threats.

MAKING DETERRENCE CREDIBLE

Credibility has two dimensions: the adversary's belief about whether or not the United States *intends* to implement its deterrence threat and the adversary's belief about whether or not the United States *can* implement that threat effectively. If either the intent or the capability is lacking, adversaries will discount U.S. deterrent threats. If both are present to a sufficient degree, U.S. deterrent threats should be highly credible. For intermediate cases in which one of these dimensions is somewhat weak, the other must (and often can) compensate.

U.S. intent has two principal facets: interests and reputation. In general, U.S. interests in a region are evidenced by political, economic, and military ties between the United States and a regional ally or friend. Efforts to convince regional opponents that the United States does, in fact, have important interests at stake in a particular region should have substantial deterrence benefits. However, for an adversary to believe that the United States is committed to the defense of a particular interest, this commitment must be exceptional, selective, and established over time—often at considerable expense (both financially and politically). Therefore, in many regional crises, the United States may not have an existing commitment to rely on for credibility.

For those many cases in which a strong commitment is lacking (at least, from the adversary's perspective) a U.S. reputation for doing what it says it will do can buttress the credibility of U.S. deterrent threats. However, reputation quickly decays and appears to be specific to a given leader (e.g., a given U.S. administration), a particular type of interest (e.g., oil), and a particular type of warfare (e.g., armored desert warfare). Thus, after Operation Desert Storm, the U.S. reputation for defending oil interests in the Middle East from conventional attack was very high. However, this reputation probably does not extend to Bosnia or Somalia, situations in which the interests and the type of military conflict are very different.

Besides interests and reputation, two lesser factors—bargaining tactics and perceptions of legitimacy—also influence the perception of a state's resolve to act in defense of some interest. To some extent, these factors simply amplify the perception of interests and reputation. However, they also can be quite distinct. For example, bargaining tactics might involve shaping events so the opponent believes only he has the "last clear chance" to avoid a confrontation. This increases the credibility of U.S. deterrent threats, because they begin to appear automatic.

The perceived legitimacy of the defender's interests, or of his methods of defense, may also affect perceptions of resolve. If the challenger believes the defender's claim to some interest is legitimate, or that his own claim is less legitimate, the challenger is likely to believe the defender has greater resolve in defending that claim. The notion of legitimacy can also be applied to the methods used to defend interests.   Certain types of weapons (e.g., chemical and biological weapons) or certain types of warfare (e.g., terrorism) may be perceived by the international community to be illegitimate for advancing a state's interests. To the extent this is true, the challenger will believe the defender has greater resolve to deter such threats. Note that the challenger does not have to agree with the defender's perspective that certain claims or means are illegitimate. All that is required is that the challenger believe the defender holds these beliefs. However, since many potential Third World advesaries hold views on legitimacy different from those of the United States, it may be difficult for such adversaries to perceive accurately the strength of U.S. views.

For these reasons, the United States cannot count on the adversary being sufficiently convinced by U.S. commitment, reputation, or claims of legitimacy. To strengthen deterrence, the United States must depend upon a robust set of effective military capabilities to offset these deficiencies.

MILITARY REQUIREMENTS FOR DETERRENCE

When they resort to force, regional adversaries typically seek short, cheap wars. Therefore, those U.S. military forces that can credibly deny a quick, decisive victory will be most impressive to the opponent. In other words, *it is those forces that are in the region, or that can deploy to the region on short notice, that will have the greatest deterrent effect.* In addition, for conventional threats, U.S. conventional forces are more relevant for regional deterrence than U.S. nuclear forces, because nuclear threats are likely to be less credible to regional adversaries—at least, so long as the adversary threatens to employ only conventional forces. While slower-arriving U.S. conventional forces can provide very effective warfighting capabilities for rolling back the adversary at a later time, they are less relevant for deterrence. Regional adversaries often do not believe such forces will arrive—although, if the adversary is threatening a target to which the United States has a credible commitment, the strength of this commitment may overcome the lower credibility of later-arriving forces.

The fact that the United States probably is limited largely to conventional forces creates problems, because, all else being equal, conventional weapons are inherently less deterring than nuclear weapons. In large part, this is due to the greater unpredictability in the performance of conventional forces. No one can be certain what will happen when conventional forces fight. This uncertainty permits adversaries to misestimate the strength of their positions. Nuclear forces are more transparent. To enhance the effectiveness of conventional forces for deterrence, the United States could improve the transparency of its prompt-denial capabilities through frequent demonstrations aimed at specific adversaries. In addition, the United States may wish to retain a nuclear element in its regional deterrence strategy, particularly—although not exclusively—to deter attacks from weapons of mass destruction.

Beyond prompt denial, the United States should incorporate punishment into its regional deterrence strategy to convince regional opponents that they will be substantially worse off if they threaten U.S. regional interests. Punishment strategies aim to threaten that which the adversary values most. For many regional adversaries, this is the leader's life or the regime's hold on power. But threatening to kill a state's leadership poses operational, moral, legal, and political problems for the United States. Therefore, the preferred strategy would be to threaten the regime's hold on power by exacerbating internal threats or increasing the opponent's vulnerability to external threats. To implement this threat, U.S. targeting could focus on selected elements of the opponent's military and internal security forces, as well as on key regime supporters (e.g., prominent industrialists, wealthy oligarchs, etc.) who help keep the regime in power.

U.S. DETERRENCE STRATEGY

For the more highly motivated regional adversaries, deterrence is likely to succeed if the United States adopts a national military strategy based on the ability to deny promptly the opponent's political and military objectives, either by basing U.S. forces within the region in times of crisis or by convincing the adversary that those forces can be forward deployed rapidly if the need arises. In addition, the United States should consider options to punish the regime by threatening to cripple its hold on power. Both punishment and denial threats must be credible—a requirement that depends on visible U.S. commitments, the U.S. reputation with respect to the particular interests at stake, and the perceived legitimacy of U.S. ends and means, as well as on the opponent's understanding of the U.S. military capabilities that can be brought to bear if U.S. leaders decide to act.

However, this begs the larger question of whether or not the United States can or should attempt to implement regional deterrence strategies. Political constraints may limit the U.S. ability and desire to implement regional deterrence successfully. Military constraints may also limit the U.S. ability to implement a robust regional deterrence strategy. In particular,

- The importance of prompt denial for deterrence runs counter to the current trend toward withdrawing U.S. forces to the continental United States and decreased readiness rates.

- The emphasis on frequent demonstrations and exercises of U.S. conventional military capabilities runs counter to the reduced operational tempo resulting from budget cutbacks.

- The emphasis on conventional forces is counter to the attractive features of U.S. nuclear escalation options, particularly for deterring nuclear, biological, or chemical attacks.

There are good reasons why these current military trends are occurring. The point to note is that, in many respects, they run counter to the requirements for an effective U.S. regional deterrence strategy.

Thus, in the post–Cold War world, can or should the United States base its regional military strategy on deterrence? During the Cold War, the United States had little choice but to accept deterrence as the only viable strategy for dealing with the Soviet nuclear threat. Now the United States has a choice. Considering the effort required to deter the hard-to-deter adversaries, the United States needs to be very selective as to where it devotes its military resources for deterrence. Therefore, at any given moment, the United States can reliably deter only a few of these adversaries, although there likely will be many more to be deterred.

ACKNOWLEDGMENTS

The authors would like to thank the following individuals for their thoughtful comments and discussions regarding regional deterrence: Marcy Agmon, John Arquilla, Christopher Bowie, Paul Davis, Yoav Ben Horin, Bruce Hoffman, Hein Goemans, Mary Morris, Brian Nichiporuk, Benjamin Schwarz, Russell Shaver, Bradley Thayer, and Nicholas K. J. Witney. Of course, credit for any errors or oddities of interpretation that remain belongs exclusively to the authors.

Chapter One

INTRODUCTION

Deterrence may well become the centerpiece of U.S. regional defense strategy. But this is by no means certain. Much is different now that the Soviet Union has faded as the primary U.S. adversary. Some of these differences may affect considerably the priority given to deterrence as an instrument of policy. For example, most potential regional adversaries of the United States will not possess nuclear weapons, at least not for awhile. Of those that do possess nuclear weapons, virtually all of them would have trouble delivering them to the United States.[1] Regional targets are more likely. Since the United States has pledged not to threaten nonnuclear states with nuclear attack, U.S. regional deterrence will take on largely a conventional character. The relative invulnerability of the United States means that warfighting is less perilous now for the United States than it was during the Cold War. In the post–Cold War era, potential U.S. adversaries will no longer be backed by a state (i.e., the former Soviet Union) posing a strategic threat to the U.S. homeland. Therefore, although conflict may be as distasteful as ever, it is not as dangerous to the United States overall. It follows that deterrence of regional adversaries is less critical to U.S. security than was deterrence of the former Soviet Union. In other words, deterrence is no longer a necessity; it is an *option* to be evaluated just like any other policy option. At the very least, the costs of mounting a credible deterrent

---

[1]"Bombs on freighters," etc., are always possible. However, we believe (and discuss below) that the operational problems posed by these modes of delivery are quite significant.

threat have to be compared to the costs of fighting a regional adversary.

This report does not contain a reformulation of deterrence theory *per se*. Deterrence theory is too generic to require reformulation. However, the way deterrence theory is *applied* to strategic policy may need reformulation to reflect the many differences between the Cold War and post–Cold War periods. Using historical case studies as a guide, and logic where systematic case studies are few, this research sought accurate generalizations about the conditions that appear to correlate with successful extended deterrence. The document is organized as follows:

- Chapter Two introduces the definition and conceptual framework we found useful for discussing regional deterrence.

- Chapter Three discusses the character and motivations of many Third World states, leading to an understanding of the circumstances under which regional deterrence may be difficult.

- Chapter Four discusses the ways in which U.S. deterrent threats can be made credible.

- Chapter Five examines the military dimensions of deterrence, with an eye toward identifying those capabilities that have the greatest impact on deterrence success.

- Chapter Six provides general observations regarding the feasibility of a U.S. regional deterrence strategy in light of the political and military constraints the United States will likely face in the coming years.

A companion document applies the reformulation of deterrence discussed here to the specific question of how the United States might deter the use of nuclear weapons against the U.S. homeland, U.S. forces overseas, or U.S. allies and friends (see Wilkening and Watman, 1994). This issue is central to the ongoing "counterproliferation" debate. This companion document specifically develops a framework for thinking about regional nuclear deterrence based on an understanding of the opponent's motivations for making nuclear threats, then discusses the basic elements of a coherent U.S. strategy for coping with the threat, including the role played by different generic classes of military capability (i.e., conventional retaliatory options, nuclear retaliatory options, active and passive defenses, and counterforce capabilities).

CONTRASTING REGIONAL DETERRENCE WITH COLD WAR DETERRENCE

There are substantial reasons to suspect, *a priori*, that the most effective strategies for deterring regional adversaries from threatening U.S. interests may be different from the U.S. deterrence strategy directed at the Soviet Union during the Cold War. This is because many fundamental assumptions about conflict with the Soviet Union, which underpinned U.S. deterrence, may not hold when deterrence is applied for very different purposes against very different types of states or regimes.

The assumptions behind deterrence of the Soviet Union can be sorted into three categories: those arising from the character and motivations of the Soviet regime, those arising from the magnitude of U.S. interests at stake in the Cold War, and those arising from the military capabilities deemed important for deterrence of the Soviet Union. In each of these areas, regional adversaries may prove to be quite different from the former Soviet Union.

The Character and Motivations of U.S. Adversaries

First, the United States assumed the Soviet leadership understood the dangers and capabilities of modern war and weapons, especially nuclear weapons (see Freedman, 1983, pp. 257–272). This assumption was based on the experience of the Soviet Union in World War II and the fact that they possessed modern weapons. The Soviets had tested nuclear weapons, were familiar with their power, and wrote extensively about their properties. Therefore, the United States had little concern that a deterrent strategy based on nuclear weapons would be minimized by the Soviet leadership. Indeed, on those occasions when the United States encountered opponents who did minimize the power of nuclear weapons, both the United States and the Soviets were alarmed, as with Mainland China in the 1950s and Cuba during the 1962 Missile Crisis.

By contrast, the leaders of many Third World states may not have a good understanding of modern military capabilities, especially the advanced conventional weapons fielded in the last decade or so.[2] These leaders do not possess such capabilities, and they have had relatively little exposure to them. Indeed, the ultimate capabilities of conventional weapons are not clear to many advanced militaries as well. We are at the opening stages of the so-called "Military-Technical Revolution," and it is well to remember that U.S. estimates of casualties for the war with Iraq numbered in the many thousands. In other words, in some ways, the U.S. performance in that campaign proved a surprise to U.S. strategists, as well as to Saddam Hussein. With the introduction of many new types of systems, a prolonged period of learning may be necessary before the full capabilities of modern forces can be absorbed.

Second, the United States assumed that the Soviet leadership valued the Soviet population and economy.[3] One component of this value was military and instrumental. It required a labor force and industrial base to produce and sustain national power. But the United States also assumed that the Soviet leadership felt some responsibility for the welfare of the Soviet people and that the future of the Soviet Union as a model to be emulated mattered. In a word, the United States assumed that the Soviet leadership was in some sense "patriotic." Therefore, the United States felt it would be effective to base its deterrent strategy, in part, on a threat to destroy large portions of the Soviet population and economy. Precisely because this threat was assumed to be catastrophic to the Soviet leadership, it was seen as the last resort of U.S. nuclear deterrence strategy.

---

[2]This is not to say that *all* Third World leaders are ignorant of the capabilities of *all* modern military forces *all* the time. It is to say that less-advanced military states are less likely to comprehend fully the capabilities of the most modern forces than the states that possess those forces. Certainly, Assad of Syria is likely to know a good deal, but his military lacks many of the capabilities that make U.S. forces so potent: advanced C^3I, effective air-to-ground weapons, stealth, and the like. Similarly, Mao knew a great deal about the powers of certain operational concepts, such as "People's War." But he grossly underestimated the capabilities of modern firepower to offset quantitative and morale factors and tactical adroitness in the Korean War. Similarly, he was markedly ignorant of nuclear weapons. On this latter point, see Freedman (1983), pp. 273–282.

[3]For discussion of this point, see Mandelbaum (1979) and Kaplan (1981), pp. 667–677.

For many Third World regimes, there may be little analogous sense of responsibility or duty toward the population and its welfare. At best, the population and civilian economy are instrumental goods for such regimes. They are valued and protected only insofar as they are important to accomplishing the goals of the regime or individual leaders. More often, the population and civilian economy are viewed with suspicion, a necessary evil unavoidable in the process of holding national power. Such leaders regard their states more as a private preserve than a personal trust. As a result, deterrence based on threats to these populations and economies may be without much coercive power. One must be skeptical that threats to destroy the civilian electric power grid would have been very effective against Papa Doc Duvalier or Idi Amin.[4] Similarly, the economic measures imposed on Haiti and Serbia have been slow to take effect, because they create pain for a group toward which the leadership is largely indifferent. This would be different if such pain created political instability that seriously threatened the leadership. While the popular welfare *per se* may not be a high priority to these leaders, retention of political power is. However, these regimes are very skilled in repressing domestic threats to themselves. This point is explored in depth in Chapter Three.

Third, throughout most of the Cold War, U.S. strategy was based on the assumption that the Soviet Union was satisfied enough with its status quo and its future prospects that it would not run great risks that might jeopardize them. This notion is captured in the description of the Soviets as "opportunistic," "conservative," or "risk averse."[5] It meant that the Soviets would exploit opportunities, but would be much less likely to embark deliberately on a course of action carrying a high risk of substantial loss.

---

[4]This is not to say that punishment as a tool of deterrence is without merit, only that traditional countervalue approaches are likely to be less effective. Attacks on targets of special interest to national leaders may have merit, as discussed in Chapter Five.

[5]The deterrence literature on communication, generally, and signaling, in particular, is quite large. Much of it is controversial, since, for many, it has become synonymous with "gradualism" or using military force indecisively. As is so often the case, the original ideas are much richer and more nuanced than are the later recollections of them. We will cite only a few of the contributions that deserve mention. See Schelling (1963); Kahn (1965); Halperin (1963), pp. 95–112; Freedman (1983), pp. 173–219.

Another indication of this view was the U.S. focus on inadvertent war, arising out of crises, as the most likely source of war rather than deliberate, premeditated aggression *à la* Nazi Germany. This meant that deterrence had to address crisis interactions, an emphasis that led to concerns about crisis stability and crisis communication. The focus on crisis decisionmaking, as opposed to premeditated plans to attack, also led to the use of so-called "signals" as a means of communication (see Halperin, 1963, pp. 95–112, and Freedman, 1983, pp. 173–219). Signals connoted military actions that themselves had little military effect on the adversary but were meant to communicate an intention and/or demonstrate a capability. Against an adversary following a deliberate plan, which presumably would take intentions and capabilities into account, signals could be expected to have little effect, except to make clear that surprise had been lost. However, in a crisis in which adversaries are attempting to communicate commitments to protect their interests, signals could convey useful information, especially nuclear signals.

Unlike the Soviet Union, many Third World states may be chronically dissatisfied with their status quo and its future prospects. That dissatisfaction may arise from many sources, but primarily it is related directly or indirectly to the unequal distribution of power, status, and resources in the international system. Such dissatisfaction may be of particular relevance to deterrence because, as is discussed in Chapters Two and Three, a belief that one's status quo and prospects are marginal can be associated with a propensity for risk-taking. By definition, states willing to accept risks are more difficult to deter, other things being equal.

The U.S. Interests at Stake

Classical deterrence theory has long stressed the importance of strength of interests as a means of making deterrence threats credible to an adversary. During the Cold War, U.S. retaliatory threats to deter Soviet nuclear attack against the United States were deemed to be highly credible because the interests at stake could not have been greater for the United States. Even when extending deterrence to protect Western Europe from a Soviet conventional attack, the U.S. interests at stake made what to many appeared to be an irrational threat (the willingness to risk the loss of New York to save Paris) appear not incredible. NATO grappled with this so-called "coupling" problem from the beginning of the alliance with much anxiety during those periods of apparent loosening between the United States and Western Europe. However, while there was disagreement over questions of degree, most analysts felt that NATO's "threat [U.S. nuclear first use] that left something to chance" could be less than completely credible and still be successful, because the Soviet leaders could never be convinced that the United States would not escalate to nuclear first use given the stakes involved—despite the vulnerability of the U.S. homeland to Soviet retaliatory strikes.[6] This point dovetails with the Soviet Union's relative satisfaction with the *status quo* throughout most of the Cold War. U.S. credibility could be less than perfect, because Soviet risk-taking propensities were relatively low, and because nuclear employment was possible, if not likely.

By contrast, in almost all regional crises, threats to U.S. national interests will not be of similar magnitude. This suggests that the United States may find it more difficult to use strength of interests to bolster the credibility of deterrence in the eyes of an adversary. If so, deterrence threats from which the United States might suffer more than a trivial cost should be especially affected. Cost is meant here in all its senses: time, resources, casualties, political support, and the like. The problem may be exacerbated by the fact that nuclear weapons frequently will not be the weapon of choice for U.S. deterrent threats. Conventional forces, though more credible, may not appear sufficiently threatening to deter regional adversaries. This takes the discussion to the military requirements for effective regional deterrence.

U.S. Military Forces for Deterrence

The military balance vis à vis the former Soviet Union focused largely on nuclear weapons. Although the basis of military stability with the former Soviet Union was not exclusively nuclear, the nuclear com-

---

[6]Though it is impossible to know what the Soviets believed, many U.S. and European analysts commented on the credibility problems inherent in NATO's strategy of flexible response. The existence of independent French and British nuclear deterrent forces eased the U.S. extended deterrence credibility problem, because Soviet leaders then had to contend with two additional paths by which nuclear war could arise out of conventional conflict in Europe. See, for example, Schwartz (1983).

ponent of any military crisis between the two superpowers made the Soviets conservative and cautious to a degree that would not likely have been achieved had the balance been entirely conventional. Several consequences for deterrence flowed from this state of affairs.

First, nuclear weapons existed in such numbers and were so overwhelming in their effect that neither side had to be terribly concerned about being able to destroy only the correct targets or, indeed, knowing with much certainty what the correct targets were. Since the early 1970s, each side could attack virtually all important target sets, though not necessarily as effectively as each would have liked (e.g., ICBM silos). The point is that the enormous destructiveness of nuclear weapons compensated for uncertainty about what the exact requirements of deterrence were.[7]

Second, nuclear weapons required no special competence to use effectively. A successful attack was almost entirely a matter of technology functioning properly. Therefore, each adversary could pin little hope on the prospect of avoiding destruction because of the incompetence of the other side, inferior generalship, lack of unit cohesion, and all of the other myriad ways in which the employment of conventional forces can be unpredictable. Therefore, military balances based on nuclear weapons are reasonably calculable, and adversaries can realistically contemplate the consequences of their use.

For deterrence of regional adversaries, the United States will have to rely largely on conventional weapons, at least in response to conventional threats. Conventional forces lack some of the fearsomeness and certainty of nuclear weapons. They may require considerable skill and resources to deploy. They may not function as hoped; unit cohesion may be low; generalship may be poor; and so on. In sum, the outcome of using conventional forces is much less predictable than the outcome of using nuclear weapons. Therefore, the magnitude of a U.S. deterrence threat based on conventional weapons may be difficult for an adversary to determine. This, in

---

[7]Of course, many arguments occurred throughout the 1970s and early 1980s about the requirements for nuclear deterrence. However, we regard these as arguments "on the margin," with national leaders on both sides essentially believing that mutual deterrence was overwhelming.

turn, suggests that conventional deterrence is likely to be less reliable than nuclear deterrence.

METHODOLOGY

These differences between deterring the former Soviet Union and deterring regional adversaries provide a basis for the questions explored in this study:

- What is the relationship between the character and motivations of the political regimes of regional adversaries, and how difficult or easy is it to deter them?

- How can deterrent threats be made credible to such adversaries when the U.S. interests at stake are likely to be less than vital?

- What military capabilities are most important for deterring regional adversaries?

To answer these questions, we relied on historical investigations of about 30 military crises between states in the 20th century. Thus, the conclusions reached are most pertinent to the problem of deterring regional states in crises that involve primarily military threats. By "regional states," we mean the political regimes governing potential Third World adversaries. We have not studied cases that focused on deterrence of nonstate actors (e.g., terrorist groups). States control territory and population. States are more-or-less fixed, organized entities with resources and values that can be threatened. Nonstate actors have a much less tangible existence. No doubt they have resources and values that they would resist losing, but these resources and values are likely to be different from those of states.

By "crises" we mean sharp, sudden increases in threat to an important U.S. national interest. Crises are often characterized by some degree of surprise and time pressure on U.S. leaders to act. The national interests endangered need not always be "vital," but they must be important enough that military responses are contemplated. Crises should be distinguished from chronic, slower-arising problems that also may involve deterrence issues.

By "military threats," we mean that, in the cases we examined, military capabilities were the primary method for threatening and deterring. Obviously, many nonmilitary instruments, such as economic sanctions, can also be used for deterrence, but this study did not examine cases in which they were major elements.

As a result of these limits on the data we used, our findings do not directly address the problem of deterring nonstate adversaries, deterrence in noncrisis circumstances, or deterrence situations emphasizing nonmilitary threats and responses. For example, we have not examined directly the requirements for deterring a state from embarking on a long-term program to acquire weapons of mass destruction. This is a chronic rather than an acute problem. Similarly, we have not dealt with deterrence of terrorists or drug cartels. Finally, we have not included evaluations of the deterrence effectiveness of nonmilitary capabilities. We understand fully the importance of these unexamined varieties of deterrence. However, for the purposes of this study, we wished to stay as close as possible to the historical data on deterrence.

A large case study–based academic literature on deterrence exists, and we have made considerable use of it.[8] In addition, we evaluated in particular detail the cases listed in Table 1. Where case studies already existed with the necessary detail and proper focus, we did not do additional historical research. We chose these 32 cases because they involved a large variety of regime types, objectives, and circumstances. Individual case studies of the crises marked with asterisks are included in this document to support particular points.

Necessarily, the process of using historical evidence is interpretive and is focused on the central tendencies that emerged from a large number of historical cases. This means that, for every broad conclusion we reach, there will be exceptions, perhaps important ones. These should be regarded as deviations around the mean—a part of any work that attempts to generalize from disparate behavior to arrive at usable findings. Readers undoubtedly will disagree with

---

[8]George (1991); Jervis, Lebow, and Stein (1985); Lebow (1981); Jervis (1976); George and Smoke (1974); Huth and Russett (1984), pp. 496, 526; Huth (1988); Huth and Russett (1988); Shimshoni (1988); Huth and Russett (1988), pp. 29–45; Huth and Russett (1990), pp. 466–501; Huth and Russett (1993); Stein (1987), 326–352; Maoz (1983), 195–230; Levy (1988).

Table 1

Historical Cases Used in This Study

1	Fashoda crisis between Britain and France (1898)
2	Morocco crisis between France and Germany (1905–1906)
3	Bosnian crisis between Austria, Britain, Russia, Serbia, and Turkey (1908–1909)
4	Agadir crisis between France and Germany (1911)
5	Austro-Serbian crisis (1914)
6	Japan's attack on the United States (1941)*
7	Iran crisis between the United States and the Soviet Union (1945–1946)
8	Berlin blockade crisis (1948)
9	Chinese invasion of Taiwan (1950)
10	North Korean invasion of South Korea (1950)
11	Chinese intervention into North Korea (1950)*
12	Chinese seizure of Quemoy-Matsu (1954, 1958)
13	The Suez crisis (1956)
14	Eisenhower Doctrine crisis in Syria (1957–1958)*
15	North Vietnamese threatened invasion of Laos (1961)
16	Iraqi-threatened invasion of Kuwait (1961)
17	The Sino-Indian war (1962)*
18	Cuban Missile Crisis (1962)
19	North Vietnamese invasion of South Vietnam (1965)
20	The Six-Day War (1967)*
21	Sino-Soviet crisis (1969)
22	Arab-Israeli War of Attrition (1969–1970)
23	The Jordanian crisis (1970)*
24	India's war with Pakistan (1971)
25	Yom Kippur War (1973)
26	Turkish invasion of Cyprus (1974)
27	Moroccan invasion of the Spanish Sahara (1975)
28	The Chinese attack on Vietnam (1979)
29	The Iran-Iraq war (1980–1988)
30	The Libyan intervention in Chad (1980, 1983)*
31	The Falklands War (1982)*
32	Iraq's invasion of Kuwait and the Gulf War (1990–1991)*

*Individual case studies included in this report.

some of our interpretations of particular cases. Such disagreements are an unavoidable consequence of the measurement problems posed in any study using historical cases. To the extent possible, we have tried to minimize the impact of differing opinions by adopting what we take to be the consensus, or majority, view of each case.[9]

As mentioned, the next two chapters discuss deterrence generally and its relationship to the characters of many Third World regimes. The logic of the argument made in these chapters is as follows:

1. Deterrence is a threat intended to inhibit a decisionmaker (in this case, an adversary's leadership) from taking a particular action.

2. Deterrence is successful when the utility of not taking that action can be made greater than the utility of taking it in the eyes of the adversary.

3. However, an area of decision theory known as "prospect theory" suggests that it is especially hard to deter a decisionmaker when inaction carries the high risk of serious loss, even when acting in the face of a deterrence threat that also carries serious risks.

4. Regional adversaries, more than the Soviet Union and the United States, are likely to find themselves confronted by situations in which the costs of inaction are deemed to exceed the costs of defying deterrence.

5. This is because, for these regimes, not to act in an international crisis often endangers the political survival of the leadership.

6. For this reason, many regional adversaries are likely to be hard to deter.

7. However, there is no evidence that many are literally "non-deterrable" or "crazy," although they may take risks that U.S. leaders would view as irrational from the U.S. perspective.

---

[9]For more information about the place of historical data in this research, see Appendix A.

Chapter Two

A CONCEPTUAL FRAMEWORK FOR DETERRENCE

Although deterrence is a familiar concept, it is worthwhile making clear precisely what we mean. Broadly defined, deterrence involves dissuading a leader, group, or state from acting against another's interests by threatening to impose some sanction or cost. At this level, deterrence applies equally well to individual behavior and to the behavior between states. Deterrence, thus defined, is part of a larger set of strategies for influencing a country's behavior. In general, one can dissuade an opponent from acting against one's interests by offering rewards or inducements if the opponent acts according to one's wishes, or by threatening sanctions or retaliation if the opponent does not. The latter is the domain of deterrence. The actions one wants to discourage can range from the acquisition of particular weapons to overt military attacks. This report focuses on the restricted set of proscribed actions in which a hostile regional power threatens to use military force against a U.S. ally or regional interest.

DEFINITIONS

Before we introduce the conceptual framework we used for deterrence, several distinctions should be made. The first is between "general" and "immediate" deterrence (see Morgan, 1983, Ch. 2). General deterrence refers to an interaction between rival states in which one state deters aggressive moves by another simply by maintaining the capability to retaliate, even though overt retaliatory threats are not made. One can say that a state of "general deterrence" exists between these two rivals, because, if not for the costs, crises involving overt threats might occur. These rivals may experience an intense arms competition, or a cold war, but overt military threats are presumably deterred. On the other hand, crises or wars might occur between two rival countries if the military balance favors one of the contestants. The appearance of crises between rival states involving overt military threats signals a breakdown of general deterrence.

Immediate deterrence, on the other hand, refers to situations in which the threat to use military force has been made explicitly, usually accompanied by visible military preparations, and the defender actively and visibly engages in attempts to dissuade the opponent from carrying out the attack by threatening some form of reprisal. In fact, a continuum of deterrence situations actually exists between general and immediate deterrence, depending on the degree of hostile intent on the part of the putative attacker and the level of visible military activity associated with the attacker's and defender's threats. With the focus on crises, this research obviously addresses immediate and not general deterrence.

The distinction between general and immediate deterrence is important for historical case studies, because accurate data are much harder to collect on the former than on the latter. Historical cases in which war did not occur are not examples of general deterrence successes if the "attacker" never intended to attack in the first place. Similarly, conflicts may not be examples of general deterrence failure if the defender never attempts to deter the attacker. Unless one can make these distinctions accurately, historical studies of general deterrence will be contaminated with false positives and false negatives, i.e., cases in which general deterrence supposedly worked or failed, when in fact deterrence either was not required or was never attempted. For this reason, most historical investigations focus on the smaller set of deterrence interactions involving immediate deterrence. By definition, immediate deterrence is easier to identify, because overt threats as well as overt military actions are taken by the putative attacker. Similarly, the defender has made overt and clear attempts to deter the attack by threatening some form of retaliation (otherwise we, again, would have a failure to attempt deterrence as opposed to a failure of deterrence). Thus, for example, it is difficult to tell whether general deterrence was successful between the United States and the former Soviet Union from 1970 to 1990. However, it is easier to tell whether immediate deterrence was successful in dissuading the Soviets from attacking Berlin in 1961. (Even here, there is disagreement about whether the Soviets actually intended to attack Berlin in 1961 or whether it was a bluff designed to extract concessions from the West short of war.)

The second distinction is between central and extended deterrence. Central deterrence refers to attempts to discourage attacks upon the deterrer's homeland, e.g., dissuading Soviet nuclear attacks against the United States during the Cold War. Similarly, Israeli attempts to dissuade Egypt or Syria from attacking Israel involve central deterrence. Extended deterrence, on the other hand, involves an interaction between three countries, labeled here as the *attacker*, the *defender*, and the *ally*. By *ally*, we mean any state the defender attempts to protect, even if there is no formal alliance between them. In fact, the defender and ally may not even be friends, as in the "Black September" incident, when Israel extended deterrence to protect Jordan from a Syrian attack in 1970.[1] The classic example of extended deterrence during the Cold War was the U.S. commitment to protect Western Europe from a conventional invasion by the Warsaw Pact. Similarly, the United States provided extended deterrence to Japan, as well as to allies in the Middle East, from possible Soviet threats.

Having made this distinction, one should note that future U.S. strategies to deter regional adversaries will principally involve extended deterrence. Military threats to the U.S. homeland will usually be absent, because regional powers lack the capability to reach the United States, with the exception of state-sponsored terrorism and perhaps the unconventional delivery of weapons of mass destruction (though this may be less likely than is often assumed).

---

[1]The Syrians invaded northern Jordan to pressure King Hussein to allow greater freedom of action for the Fedayeen (a radical Palestinian guerrilla movement) then operating out of Jordan. Since Jordan was in the midst of a civil war, King Hussein clamped down on operations of the Fedayeen. Israel supported Jordan's efforts to limit Fedayeen activities and, hence, wanted to deter further Syrian pressure. Israel's retaliatory threat consisted of verbal warnings accompanied by the forward deployment of armored forces along the Israel-Jordan border. Under the threat of Israeli intervention, Syria ultimately withdrew from northern Jordan, allowing King Hussein to prevail. This is also a clear case of immediate, as opposed to general, deterrence. For more detail, see the discussion of the Jordanian historical case (1970) in Chapter Five.

Finally, it is important to distinguish between deterrence by denial and deterrence by punishment.[2] Deterrence by denial attempts to dissuade an adversary from attacking by convincing him that he cannot accomplish his political and military objectives with the use of force or that the probability of accomplishing his political and military objectives at an acceptable cost is very low. In general, deterrence by denial threatens the opponent's military forces, especially those capable of projecting power beyond the opponent's borders. Thus, it is frequently referred to as a "countermilitary" deterrent strategy. In many respects, deterrence by denial is similar to the concept of "direct defense," i.e., physically blocking an attack, with the emphasis on dissuading an opponent as opposed to using brute force to block the attack.

Deterrence by punishment attempts to dissuade an opponent from attacking by threatening to destroy or otherwise take away that which the opponent values. For this reason, it is frequently called a "countervalue" deterrent strategy. One way to do this is to threaten civilian economic targets. But punishment can involve a much broader range of targets, including such values as an adversary's foreign presence or economic interests and its political structure. These value targets may or may not include the opponent's military forces. The emphasis here is not on denying the opponent's military objectives, but rather on inflicting sufficient pain to outweigh any benefits the adversary hopes to gain by attacking.[3]

Deterrence by denial and deterrence by punishment are, of course, pure types. Actual strategies incorporate elements of both to varying degrees, depending on which type of threat is believed to be most credible and most effective for a given adversary. Nevertheless, it is useful to talk about them separately, because they have quite different targeting implications.

RATIONAL CHOICE THEORY

Our approach to deterrence rests on rational choice theory, although the language of expected utility models (one variant of a rational

---

[2]For a discussion of this point see Snyder (1961).

[3]See Davis (1994).

choice approach) is useful for discussing the mechanics of deterrence. Expected utility theory makes several assumptions about the decisionmaker's ability to collect and weigh information, develop alternatives, assign utilities to them, and assess probabilities so a decision can ultimately be made by choosing the option from among the alternatives that maximizes the expected utility.[4] Expected utility theory requires all of these assumptions to be true and is invalidated when they are not.[5]

Rational choice, on the other hand, might be called an "approach," a "framework," or a way of thinking about decisionmaking (see Elster, 1986). It is essentially descriptive of a decisionmaking *process* that

---

[4]Numerous publications explain the fundamental assumptions behind expected utility theory. A classic introduction can be found in Kreps (1990, Ch. 3). Other essays on the topic can be found in Eatwell, Milgate, and Newman (1990), including "Economic Theory and the Hypothesis of Rationality" by Kenneth Arrow, "Expected Utility and Mathematical Expectation" by David Schmeidler and Peter Wakker, "Expected Utility Hypothesis" by Mark Machina, "Rational Behavior" by Amartya Sen, "Subjective Probability" by I. J. Good, and "Utility Theory and Decision Theory" by Peter C. Fishburn, to name a few. For a good discussion of recent developments in expected utility theory, see Machina (1987).

[5]The purpose and adequacy of rational choice theory are much debated. Construed as equating with expected utility theory, rational choice has been strongly criticized as misrepresenting the way individuals actually make decisions. Experience and experimental evidence demonstrate that human beings do not and cannot develop and weigh probabilities and utilities with the rigor implied by expected utility theory. This line of argument has been elaborated in many instances. See, for example, Davis and Arquilla (1991a,b).

These objections to expected utility theory are legitimate. Humans bring many issues to decisionmaking that may not be represented in the theory, which is, after all, intended to be prescriptive. For this reason, we speak here of rational choice theory, not expected utility theory. Rational choice theory provides a general, qualitative description of human decisionmaking. No doubt it is incomplete, as all theories are. The question is whether rational choice theory is *so* distortive of human decisionmaking as to be useless as an organizing framework for our discussion. We think it is *not*. Simon (1958) and Kahneman and Tversky (1979), pp. 263–291, make their criticisms of the shortcomings of rational choice theory by modifying it, not eliminating it.

This is precisely the sense in which we use it. We accept fully that human rationality is bounded, as Simon argues, and that the assessment of utility and risk is filled with psychological shortcuts and distortions, as Kahneman and Tversky show so well. But these and other researchers take as their starting place that rational choice theory is an indispensable paradigm of decisionmaking, at least so far. This is because human beings do seem to think in terms of alternatives, utilities, and probabilities, even if imperfectly. And these researchers have not found those imperfections to be so great as to require abandonment of the theory as a very robust foundation on which many valuable additions can be built.

observation and experiment suggest qualitatively corresponds to the way humans actually make decisions.   This process consists of building a mental model of the future by construing decisions in terms of alternatives, predicting the expected consequences of each, and selecting the one that promises a result sufficiently close to the one desired. The way decisionmakers actually conduct this process may depart considerably from the quantitative formalism of expected utility theory.   But the qualitative content of the rational choice approach generally provides the basis for virtually all modern research in this area. For our purposes, it provides a clear way of understanding the workings of deterrence and the reasons why it succeeds or fails.

With these distinctions in mind, we now develop the conceptual framework we found useful for thinking about regional deterrence. The framework used here draws on rational choice theory. Rational choice theory can be applied to the decisionmaking of individuals, organizations, or states, provided the actor behaves in an instrumentally rational manner, i.e., chooses the option that maximizes the actor's expected utility.

Figure 1 shows a simplified decision tree for a leader contemplating an attack. This, of course, is a highly stylized representation of the choices facing leaders. More realistic decision trees would include different types of "attack" (e.g., limited probes, pressures of various sorts short of war, along with large military attacks), and multiple branches representing different responses on the part of the defender, with different probabilities associated with each response. Despite this more general formulation, the simple binary decision tree in Figure 1 is sufficient to illustrate the important elements of deterrence. We use it here to organize our thinking about regional deterrence.

Referring to Figure 1, if a leader decides to attack, there are two possible outcomes, U_1 and U_2, depending on whether or not the defender retaliates after the attack has occurred. U_1 represents the utility from the attacker's point of view of launching an attack and receiving some specified retaliation. The probability that the defender will actually retaliate is given by p. The attacker's belief that the deterrent threat is a bluff is given by $1 - p$. Finally, the value, from the attacker's perspective, of carrying out an attack without

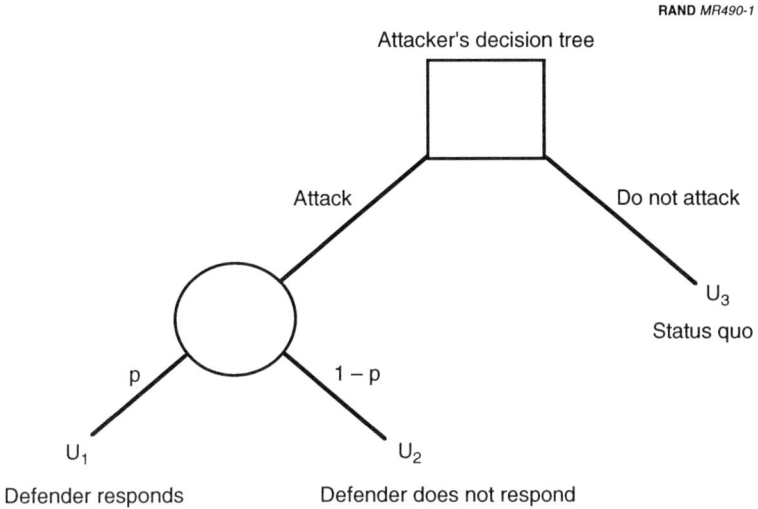

RAND *MR490-1*

Attacker's decision tree

Attack

Do not attack

U_3

Status quo

p

1 − p

U_1

U_2

Defender responds

Defender does not respond

Figure 1—Attacker's Decision Tree

drawing a response from the defender is represented by U_2. Therefore, from the attacker's point of view, the utility of attacking is given by comparing these two possible outcomes weighted by the likelihood that each will occur.

In deciding whether or not to attack, the leadership compares the expected outcome of attacking to the expected outcome of not attacking, i.e., of accepting the status quo. The utility associated with the status quo is represented by U_3 in Figure 1. The status quo includes not only the attacker's contentment with his current situation but also his evaluation of his future prospects. If the leadership believes that conditions in its country are deteriorating rapidly and that waiting will almost certainly bring about a substantial loss relative to the current situation, then U_3 is negative (even if the current status quo is acceptable). Deterrence succeeds if the expected utility of attacking is less than the expected utility of not attacking.

Using this formulation, one can readily see that deterrence does not simply involve a comparison of the costs (i.e., U_1) relative to the benefits (i.e., U_2) of attacking, as is so often stated in discussions about deterrence, but rather it involves a comparison of these costs and benefits relative to the attacker's perception of the status quo and its future prospects. When a country is facing a deteriorating status quo (i.e., the value of U_3 is negative), the expected costs have to be more negative to outweigh the expected benefits for deterrence to be effective.

If the defender's threat to retaliate is credible, the value of p is high and the attacker's decision is essentially based on a comparison of U_1 and U_3. On the other hand, if the credibility of the defender's threat is low, it is easy to see why deterrence fails, because the attacker compares U_2 (a positive outcome) to U_3 (which can be positive or negative).

At this point, one can see how the three factors examined in this study affect deterrence. The character and motivations of regional adversaries are represented by the magnitudes of U_1, U_2, and U_3.[6] The credibility of the deterrer is represented by the value of p. Finally, the military balance affects not only the credibility that the deterrer will actually carry out his threats, but also the magnitude of U_1.[7]

Including the status quo in discussions of deterrence seems like an obvious point except that it is honored more often in the breach.[8] In

---

[6]In principle, these utilities incorporate political (international and domestic), economic, and military factors. In fact, as Chapter Three discusses, domestic political considerations may be among the most important factors that affect many Third World leaders' subjective evaluations of utility. For example, leaders concerned with maintaining personal power may be sensitive to threats to target the instruments by which they maintain control of their regime (e.g., the secret police, select elements of the military). This is incorporated into U_1. Likewise, the utility associated with a successful foreign venture (i.e., U_2) may be measured largely in terms of its impact on domestic political stability. Finally, U_3 reflects the leadership's perception of the status quo and its future prospects, e.g., the regime's ability to stay in power if no action is taken.

[7]The attacker may also discount certain military capabilities. For example, if an attacker (who does not possess nuclear weapons) does not believe the defender will use nuclear weapons first because of political, strategic, or moral constraints, the credibility attached to nuclear threats is essentially zero, even though the magnitude of U_1 would be quite negative if nuclear weapons were used.

[8]See, for example, a classic formulation of deterrence by George and Smoke (1974), pp. 59–60. Although these authors leave out the status quo in discussing the basic propositions of deterrence, one suspects they are aware of its importance, because they include values for the status quo in their discussion of game theory on page 68.

fact, the opponent's view of his future prospects may be the most important factor motivating regional leaders to act. This has important implications for how hard it might be to deter certain states. If an opponent believes his current situation and the prospects for the future are so bleak that "he has nothing to lose" by acting, then the value of U_3 is negative in the extreme. If so, it will be virtually impossible to make the expected utility of attacking more negative than the value of U_3. A slight chance that the defender is bluffing will suffice to make attacking appear more attractive than not attacking.

Many people have commented on the fact that deterrence requires rational decisionmaking on the part of leaders.[9] Critics of deterrence often point to decision trees like that shown in Figure 1 to argue that decisionmakers do not possess perfect information, much less the cognitive ability to process this information in the midst of a crisis, to carry out the calculations required by expected utility theory to act in a rational manner. However, the only assumptions required by rational choice theory are that leaders develop preferences among their alternatives; that they rank their preferences ordinally, even if imperfectly; and that they choose the alternative best suited to accomplishing their objective, again even if imperfectly.[10] Even if information is sparse and cognitive limitations prevent complete digestion of the available information, this does not imply that leaders will act irrationally, i.e., choose an alternative that they believe does *not* best correspond to their objective. The subjective utilities U_1, U_2, and U_3, as well as the credibility p, may be subject to biases and distortions; however, within these bounds, leaders will still act so as to maximize the utility associated with the options they see before them. In short, most of the psychological critiques of deterrence do not invalidate the "rational actor" assumption upon which deterrence theory rests. However, they do suggest that deterrence is difficult to implement as a strategy, because the defender, in constructing his deterrent threats, must be aware of the multifaceted nature of the opponent's decision tree, as well as the psychological biases and

---

[9]For a defense of rational deterrence theory, see Achen and Snidal (1989). A series of critiques of Achen and Snidal's position is found in the same issue, namely, George and Smoke (1989), Jervis (1989), Lebow and Stein (1989), and Downs (1989).

[10]See Zagare (1990), pp. 238–260.

limitations that affect the attacker's perception of the risks associated with alternative courses of action.

PROSPECT THEORY AND DETERRENCE

Thus far, the workings of deterrence have been represented according to simple rational choice theory. Over the past several decades, researchers have observed that decisionmakers consistently treat the prospect of losses differently from the prospect for gains, though rational choice theory predicts no such distinction. Such findings have been obtained from several different disciplines: psychology, economics, and political science. An elaboration of rational choice theory known as "prospect theory" was developed to account for these observed anomalies.[11] In our judgment, the introduction of prospect theory, or more precisely the empirical observations that led to the formulation of prospect theory, enriches considerably the classical formulation of deterrence.[12] (We do not actually make use of the mathematical formalism developed by Kahneman and Tversky for prospect theory.)

Prospect theory explicitly accounts for the fact that decisionmakers appear to weigh losses more heavily than gains in ways not accounted for by comparing the apparent utilities of alternatives.[13] It is as though the concept of "loss" has a different psychological connotation than the concept of "gain," independent of the utilities involved. The result is that, all else being equal, decisionmakers usually accept greater risks to avert a loss than to achieve a gain, even when the expected utilities of the choices would predict the oppo-

---

[11]See Kahneman and Tversky (1979), pp. 263–291; Kahneman, Slovak, and Tversky (1982); and Quattrone and Tversky (1988).

[12]The application of prospect theory to conventional deterrence has also been discussed in Davis and Arquilla (1991b).

[13]Risk aversion in expected utility theory is represented by a concave utility function (i.e., one exhibiting diminishing utility with higher gains). Risk-seeking behavior, on the other hand, is represented in prospect theory by a convex utility function (i.e., one exhibiting diminishing utility for larger losses, where the utility domain has now been divided into gains and losses). When facing a choice between a certain loss and a gamble on a larger loss (where the expected loss is equal in both cases), utility is maximized by taking the gamble.

site.[14] Indeed, decisionmakers will accept particularly high risks to avert a serious or irremediable loss. This idea is captured by the phrase "the strategic costs of inaction," i.e., the costs of accepting prospective loses may be too high for leaders not to act. The distinction between these two occasions for risky decisions—opportunity to gain versus aversion of loss—helps one understand why deterrence can be difficult.

Thus, leaders facing losses can be expected to choose a course of action that runs the risk of greater losses so long as this choice contains the possibility of averting the loss. How much of a gamble depends on the risk-taking propensities of individual leaders. This risk-taking propensity is particularly acute if U_3 represents a certain loss and if the decisionmaker seeking to avert the loss already has a marginally acceptable status quo and anticipates that the impending loss will make the status quo unacceptable. Indeed, at the limit, such decisionmakers become literally nondeterrable if they believe they have nothing to lose by acting.[15] By the same token, decisionmakers seeking to improve on a status quo that is already satisfactory are easiest to deter, because they are least inclined to take risks that might jeopardize their agreeable situation.

Although this discussion is based on the crucial distinction between two seemingly dichotomous types of risk-taking situations—averting loss and seeking gain—we do not mean to imply that any decision is entirely one or the other. Rather, all decisions involve mixes of the two. The more the desire to avert loss dominates the mix, the greater the propensity for risk-taking and the harder that leader or state is to deter, other things being equal. The more the desire for gain domi-

---

[14]A risk-averse decisionmaker is one who prefers a gain with certainty to a gamble of achieving the same expected gain or perhaps even a slightly higher expected gain. A risk-prone decisionmaker is just the opposite: He prefers a gamble to a certain outcome. The reader can easily demonstrate risk aversion for gains by asking whether one would rather receive $100 for certain or gamble on a 50-50 chance of receiving $210 or nothing. Most people prefer the certain outcome of $100 over the bet, even though the bet has a slightly higher expected return, i.e., $105. On the other hand, when facing losses, most people prefer a 50-50 gamble on losing $210 to the certain loss of $100.

[15]The condemned convict awaiting execution is an appropriate example. If he is convinced that no pardon will save him, there is no sanction that will deter him from taking any risk. What threat is more fearsome and certain than the one that awaits him?

nates, the greater the propensity for risk avoidance and the easier it is to deter that type of leader.

This is represented graphically by Figure 2, which portrays the deterrence continuum. Hardest-to-deter is at the left; easiest-to-deter is at the right. Among the easiest-to-deter states are the United States and the countries of Western Europe. These are societies with relatively ample status quo's and good prospects for the future. The stakes must be very high indeed to motivate these states to undertake risky behavior. Also on the easier-to-deter side was the former Soviet Union, although it was probably further to the left than the United States. This impression was reflected in the scholarly discussions of Soviet conservatism with respect to risk-taking throughout the Cold War (see for example, Adomeit, 1986).

As we seek to show in the forthcoming discussion, many regional adversaries are likely to fall on the left or harder-to-deter side of the continuum. This is because these types of states are more likely than the United States or the Soviet Union to find themselves threatened by the risk of serious or unacceptable losses unless they act.

Note that at the leftmost end of the continuum is the point at which the cost of inaction becomes so large as to warrant accepting any risk. Such a point is reached when the magnitude and likelihood of loss are very large unless some ameliorative action is taken. In principle, this should be the realm of the "nondeterrables," states that

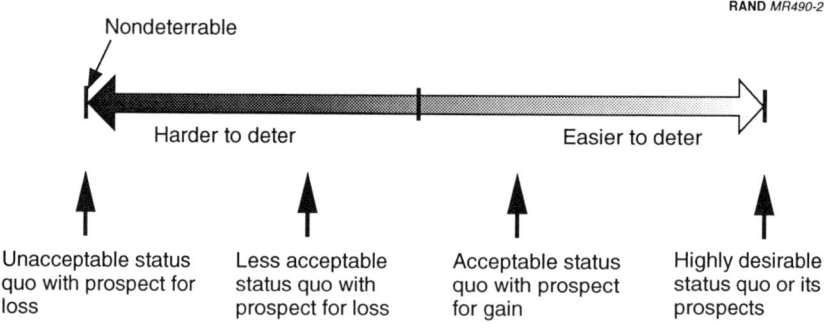

Figure 2—The Spectrum of Risk-Taking Behavior

cannot be inhibited by a threat because no threat is as costly as doing nothing.

Fortunately, we have found no evidence to suggest such states actually exist. This does not mean they have not or could not, only that we found no evidence that the theoretical possibility has been realized in the post–World War II period. It is probably safe to say that true nondeterrability is likely to be quite rare at any time, although it must be granted that North Korea and Cuba may become the latest candidates for nondeterrability status. Thus far, both have behaved as though each has something left to lose. For example, North Korea has not yet decided that its future is so grim that "rolling the dice" on a military option is preferable. Again, the next few months are likely to show whether this is because the North truly does have something left to lose or merely because its preparations are not complete.

The related notion of so-called crazy states should be mentioned here in connection with nondeterrability (see Dror, 1980). In principle, a state may be nondeterrable because it is too irrational to be sensitive to a deterrent threat. Since deterrent threats often are rather crude, this degree of irrationality has to be pronounced. Based on the cases we examined, we found very few, if any, clear examples of leaderships irrational to this degree. Many leaderships of regional states can be characterized as paranoid or perhaps sociopathic, but very few can be characterized as disabled by psychopathology. The process of competing for and holding power has much in common with rivalry between states, so the domestic political process may weed out individuals who are highly incompetent in domestic and international politics. Idi Amin of Uganda and Emperor Bokassa of the Central African Republic may be exceptions, although even their respective disabilities became pronounced only after they had held power for a time. Certainly, many highly unpleasant individuals have held power in Third World states, but few could be called crazy in the sense of being so irrational as to be nondeterrable.

Instead, we have found that regional adversaries may be hard to deter, if not nondeterrable. This leads them to accept high risks, risks that might be deemed "crazy" if the United States accepted them. But, confronted with the prospect of serious losses, seemingly crazy risk-taking can be entirely rational. The question is: Why do many regional adversaries find themselves in crises carrying the risk of serious losses, and what is the character of those losses? We believe part of the answer to this question is the way many of these states are governed, the subject of the next chapter.

Chapter Three

THE CHARACTER AND MOTIVATIONS
OF REGIONAL ADVERSARIES

REGIME TYPES

Our research on regional deterrence led us to explore the extent to which a relationship exists between the basic types of regional regimes the United States may encounter and the requirements for deterring them. To begin, we start with a taxonomy of regime types. There many ways to construct such a taxonomy.[1] We have used a simple model that distinguishes between the three basic regime types described in the literature:

(a) Democratic regimes

(b) Authoritarian regimes

(c) Totalitarian regimes.

While we have included democratic regimes for completeness, the characteristics and motivations of nondemocratic regimes are far more relevant. This is because the great majority of Third World regimes remain nondemocratic. Of those that are democratic, it is unlikely that the United States will find itself in a crisis with one in

---

[1]The following discussion draws from the large academic literature on regime types and the characteristics associated with them. We found the following work particularly helpful: Linz (1975). Those interested in surveying this field more widely should see Wiseman (1966), Almond and Coleman (1960), Almond and Powell (1966), Finer (1971), Blondel (1972), Rustow (1967), Organski (1965), Apter (1965).

which military deterrence is an issue.[2] Therefore, authoritarian, totalitarian, and personal dictatorship regimes are emphasized in this
analysis.

These regime types differ across three criteria: the amount of compulsory public participation in regime activities, the amount of pluralism or alternative sources of political power, and the extent to
which formal ideology plays a role in regime legitimacy and behavior. Compulsory public participation refers to an obligation imposed
under penalty by the state on each citizen to take an active part in
certain political activities. These might involve membership in a
political organization at the workplace or home, acting as an infor-
mant to the secret police, public demonstrations on state occasions,
participation in youth activities, etc. Degree of pluralism refers to the
extent that centers of political, economic, and social power exist
other than the central government. For example, in some regimes
the church, industrialists, union leaders, or other social institutions
may possess power independent from the state leadership. Formal
ideology refers to an elaborate code for interpreting the past and the
present and providing guidance for the future. It rationalizes the existence of the regime and enumerates the characteristics of the leadership that entitle it to rule. In the Soviet case, Marxism-Leninism
provided the intellectual underpinnings for empowering the Party
and its elite as the vanguard of the revolution, based on their supposedly superior understanding of the workings of societies.

Although often seen as interchangeable, authoritarian and totalitarian regimes differ considerably according to the three criteria listed
above, and this distinction is important for the study of deterrence.
Figure 3 illustrates these differences by locating each regime type
along the dimensions of compulsory participation, pluralism, and
ideology.

In a purely authoritarian regime, citizens are not required to partici-
pate in any regular political activities. Passive compliance with the
regime's dictates is all that is necessary. Authoritarian regimes are

---

[2]There has been a lot of scholarly discussion of the proposition that democracies do
not go to war with each other, although they show no reluctance to fight nondemocra-
cies. For a recent discussion of this argument, see Doyle (1986). For an opposing
point of view, see Layne (1993), pp. 5–51.

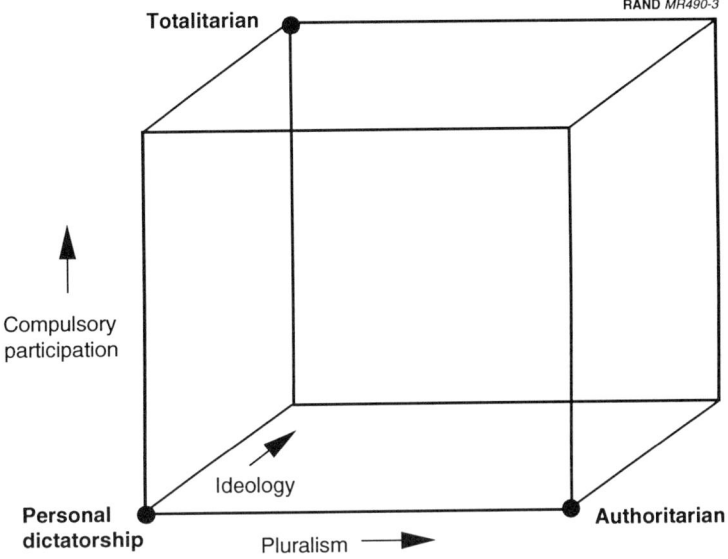

Figure 3—Regime Types

more like democracies in this way. Franco's Spain, Salazar's Portugal, and Greece under the junta are good examples. By contrast, totalitarian regimes are characterized by very strong coercive pressures on the general public to become politically involved in some way. It may be through "block committees" or "self-criticism" as in Cuba and the People's Republic of China. The various forms of public political activity may be quite minor, but, in the aggregate, the degree of social mobilization in totalitarian regimes is high compared to that in authoritarian regimes.

Authoritarian regimes are more pluralistic than totalitarian, though certainly not as pluralistic as democracies. The alternative power centers in an authoritarian society are not based on popular sovereignty. Rather, they are important elite institutions, such as the military, the religious hierarchy, the wealthy, a traditional aristocracy, and the like. These multiple power centers have a degree of independence unknown in totalitarian regimes. Authoritarian regimes do not have true monopolies of power. Rather, they must maintain themselves by political activity: accommodation, bribery, *quid pro quo,* playing rivals off against one another, and the like. Hence, authoritarian regimes are involved in constant "juggling acts" that frequently make them quite unstable. That instability is exacerbated by the permanent difficulties these regimes encounter in establishing legitimacy—in making clear why they should hold power and others should not. Ultimately, most authoritarian leaders are compelled to substitute claims of special effectiveness for legitimacy, which can be strengthened by simple longevity.[3] This point about the dynamic aspects of authoritarian regime politics is particularly important for deterrence, for it provides an explanation for the crisis behavior of these regimes and the location of targets of considerable vulnerability and sensitivity.

Totalitarian regimes have little pluralism, or there are no sources of power in such societies other than the state. Organizations may exist that have the appearance of independence, such as religious groups, labor unions, physicians, and the like. But the power they possess is entirely derivative and revocable at will by the central authority. Such regimes are usually more stable than authoritarian regimes. They are not engaged in an internal "juggling" act, because no other institutions require juggling. However, this monopoly of power is purchased by a very heavy investment in the apparatus of state coercion: secret police, domestic intelligence, the militarization of domestic life, and the like. Indeed, both totalitarian and authoritarian regimes have this emphasis on domestic security in common. In both cases, the obsession with internal security is a manifestation of the chronic problem these regimes must overcome: the precariousness of the domestic political order.

Finally, authoritarian regimes have few if any formal ideological underpinnings. They frequently exploit nationalism and xenophobia for the purposes of generating political energy. However, such regimes seldom have complex institutional structures for elaborating, communicating, and codifying these themes. References to a great national "Golden Age" may appear in speeches and pronouncements. Persecution of various stigmatized groups may be

---

[3]Presumably, any group or individual capable of holding power for a long time in such circumstances must be presumed to possess some special skills.

encouraged. But these activities have little resemblance to the systematic approach taken to ideology in totalitarian regimes.

In contrast, totalitarian regimes usually depend heavily on ideology as a source of legitimacy. Ideology refers here to a formal and elaborate set of institutions for the promulgation of political thought supportive of the regime and the education of the public in it. These institutions are often represented at the highest political levels. Individuals can pursue careers in ideological activity; academic degrees are awarded in it; and ideological institutions compete favorably for resources with the other state priorities.

In either an authoritarian or totalitarian regime, central power usually resides mainly in an individual, although that need not be so. Power could reside in a junta, such as in Greece or Argentina. Power can reside partly in an individual and partly in a council, such as in the Soviet Union after Stalin. It can reside entirely in an individual surrounded by institutions with only derivative power, such as in Stalin's Soviet Union or, perhaps, Saddam Hussein's Iraq. Power can be distributed among a strong individual and strong semiautonomous institutions, such as in Franco's Spain or Salazar's Portugal. Finally, power can reside entirely in an individual surrounded by virtually no enduring institutions, such as in Idi Amin's Uganda or Papa Doc Duvalier's Haiti.

Obviously, as with any taxonomy, so-called pure cases are rare. Indeed, they may be nonexistent. The most extreme form of totalitarian regime would be a single person who holds and wields all power. While some regimes have approached this point, we can find none that has reached it. This is because the task of governance almost always requires delegation and institution building, a process that automatically creates the possibility of alternative power centers, even weak ones. The greater the extent of this power sharing, the more the regime can be characterized as authoritarian. The majority of regimes the United States will encounter will have substantial authoritarian elements.

Stalin's Soviet Union or Kim Il Sung's North Korea may come closest to a pure totalitarian regime. What power was delegated to other institutions seems to have been entirely derivative and revocable with little cost. Compare this to Hitler's Germany, in which power

was derived, but, once delegated, led to the creation of semiautonomous institutions: the SS, the war industries, the armed forces,
and so on. It is not clear whether Hitler could have stripped
Himmler and the SS of their power. Similarly, the costs of stripping
Speer of his were deemed too high, which afforded him considerable
safety and autonomy. Further toward the authoritarian pole might
be Assad's Syria. This is a regime with strong totalitarian strains, yet
power is shared with other individuals and institutions. Or, at least,
Assad has to be concerned to maintain the support of those individuals and institutions while preventing them from growing too powerful. Less totalitarian was Nasser's Egypt. King Hussein's Jordan,
prior to the constitution, was even less so. Opinions are mixed over
where to place Saddam Hussein's Iraq along this continuum. Some
would place that regime at about the same place as Stalin's. Others
would place it close to that of Assad. Few would rate it as any less
totalitarian than that.

DOMESTIC POLITICAL INSTABILITY

These distinctions between regime characteristics are important for
deterrence. The central problem of both regime types is chronic
domestic instability—at least in the view of their leaderships.[4]
Instability refers here to the extent to which the regime's hold on
political power is precarious or fragile. One indicator of this instability is the frequency of regime changes in the developing world. But
this statistic may not be most revealing, because several regional
regimes have great longevity, for example, those in Syria, Iraq, and
North Korea. More revealing of instability are the levels of resources
and effort devoted to suppressing internal dissent. The great size of
internal security establishments is a characteristic that many otherwise dissimilar regimes share in common. Thus, the fact that some

---

[4]For an extensive discussion of the internal weaknesses of Third World states, see
Buzan (1988), pp. 14–43. Buzan proposes a regime taxonomy in which he categorizes
states as unified, fragmented, and anarchic. There is a strong correlation between totalitarian and authoritarian Third World states, on the one hand, and fragmented
states, on the other. For recent books on national security in the Third World, see
David (1991), Jackson (1993), and Job (1992).

regimes have endured is more a reflection of the leadership's skills in rooting out domestic opponents than it is the absence of opponents.[5]

What explains this chronic instability? These regimes lack the legitimacy needed to justify why (besides simple possession of power) they should rule. Many more totalitarian regimes seek to ameliorate this problem by stressing their ideological basis. But few, if any, have been able to rely on ideology alone as a durable source of legitimacy for more than a decade or two. Soviet Marxism became increasingly cynical in its dependence on naked coercion. Nazism was defeated in war less than 20 years after its accession to power. Authoritarian leaders have an even more difficult legitimacy problem, since ideology usually plays only a minor role in such regimes. Perhaps some religiously based regimes, such as Iran's, may be successful at sustaining a claim of legitimacy, although it is too early to tell. Perhaps, Nasser's regime could be said to have been based on a principle, the leadership of the Arab nationalist movement. A few authoritarian leaders may derive some legitimacy from the risks they took in earlier revolutionary activity or in their descent from important personages. But, for the most part, it is difficult to discover a single example of a Third World nondemocratic regime that succeeds in deriving legitimacy sufficient to permit doing without an extensive apparatus for sheer repression.

Greatly exacerbating this problem is the fact that most Third World states are only partially formed. They are still involved in the problems of state building that were settled in Europe and the United States by the end of the 19th century. Governance in these states is often highly personal and poorly institutionalized. Political forms, values, and systems may not survive the leadership of particular individuals. Rational bureaucracies often do not exist or exist precariously. In particular, publicly recognized and reliable arrangements for succession do not exist in many of these states.

---

[5]The F-16 fighter provides an interesting analogy to the instability of these states. The F-16 is aerodynamically unstable. Yet it does not fall out of the air, because computers make the myriad slight control adjustments necessary to keep the plane aloft. If those computers were to fail, a human pilot would quickly lose control. The fact that few F-16s crash is not an indication of their stability; it is an indication of how well their inherent instability is managed. Precisely the same is true of most Third World regimes.

These problems of illegitimacy and weak institutions tend to create more problems for authoritarian regimes. This is because authoritarian regimes are more pluralistic than totalitarian ones. Plurality can be a source of great strength in the context of a regime with widely recognized and accepted legitimacy, an established process for governance and succession, and institutions not dependent for survival on particular individuals. In the absence of these sources of stability, political plurality can be highly destabilizing, especially when the competing power centers are closely balanced. Without a respected theory of legitimacy, any individual or institution with power can seriously entertain attempting to seize control. Without strong processes controlling political competition and succession, power is accumulated through *ad hoc* arrangements of rewards and penalties. These arrangements seldom have the durability of institutions, so they rise and fall for purely tactical reasons. Such impermanence makes domestic politics fragile, especially before a regime can accumulate longevity, a proxy for legitimacy.

This fragility can be termed a chronic internal crisis. Indeed, all the security organizations of the state have as their primary mission the control of this crisis. For this reason, it is often said that the most serious threats to the national security of many Third World regimes are domestic. This should be contrasted with the Western model of national security, in which external threats are the focus of interest.

Several authors have made this observation. For example Mohammed Ayoob (1991, pp. 257–283) states that

> Security as a concept is fundamentally different for Third World States than for First World States. . . . Security for Third World States emanates from within. . . . Most leaderships are preoccupied primarily with internal threats to the security of their state structures and to the regimes themselves.

In the same vein Jusuf Wanandi (1981) writes that

> Conflicts in the Third World are basically reflections of internal weaknesses. . . . Internal weaknesses may be the result of . . . decolonization; . . . political struggles; . . . social revolution.

The emphasis on domestic threats to national security is crucial to understanding the crisis behavior of Third World states, for, in many cases, a regime's responses to those threats help propel them into international crises. This can happen in several ways, as is illustrated below in some of the case studies. For example, a regime may find an international event unacceptable, because it improves the situation of domestic enemies. This was the problem Mao tried to address when he ordered the intervention in the Korean War in 1950. A weak regime may create a crisis or seize on an international situation as an opportunity to prove its effectiveness. Argentina's junta took this course in the Falklands in 1982. A regime may enter into an international crisis unwillingly as the only way to protect itself from domestic criticism. Such was the case of Nasser in 1967 and Nehru in his conflict with China in 1962.

These threats to domestic stability can take several forms. Most frequently, the threat is to the political power or survival of the existing leadership. However, threats to the existing system of governance, to relations between important social groups, and even to the survival of the state are not uncommon either. The point is that, although the proximate cause of an international crisis involving a Third World state may be an external event, its deeper causes are often more a function of domestic threats to the weightiest interests of the leadership. The stakes could not be higher for these regimes, and they behave accordingly.

Most often, authoritarian regimes are more vulnerable to domestic crisis than totalitarian ones, because authoritarian regimes can depend less on purely repressive means to ensure control. Institutions and powerful individuals have to be co-opted on a continuing basis, and their displeasure cannot be ignored. This equilibrium of forces that permit authoritarian regimes to rule is often exquisitely sensitive. Therefore, such regimes have little internal capacity to absorb shocks to that equilibrium. Those may arise from inside or outside the state, and the leaders of such regimes have to react emphatically to them, or believe that they do. Because more totalitarian regimes do not depend so much on maintaining an equilibrium, because the power of these regimes is more unitary and centralized, they are less sensitive to internal pressures. Presumably, Stalin was less concerned about the reaction of the Soviet industrialists to his decisionmaking than Franco was about the Spanish industrialists.[6]

What follows are five of the many cases that illustrate the powerful ways in which concerns for domestic stability lead already fragile states to aggressive international risk-taking. One concerns a powerful, totalitarian regime; another a weak, partially formed totalitarian regime; two involve authoritarian regimes; and one a democratic regime. These cases are as follows:

- The Chinese decision to intervene in Korea in 1950

- Argentina's invasion of the Falkland Islands in 1982

- Egypt's decision to remilitarize the Sinai in 1967

- India's attempt to coerce the Chinese over a disputed border area in 1962

- Iraq's invasion of Kuwait in 1990.[7]

HISTORICAL CASES ILLUSTRATING THE INFLUENCE OF DOMESTIC POLITICS

China, 1950

The Chinese decision to enter the Korean War in the winter of 1950 is an excellent example of the ways in which domestic fragility can drive a state's international behavior. In addition, this decision also demonstrates the strength of motivation that results when domestic

---

[6]Clearly, democratic regimes also feel pressures to act internationally to maintain domestic strength. However, these regimes are not so sensitive to such pressures as are many nondemocratic Third World regimes. This is because a democratically elected head of state or government does not have the freedom of action of nondemocratic leaders. He or she is hemmed in by a plethora of competing institutions, as well as by the public. Therefore, while a president or prime minister may want desperately to serve his or her own political interests in a particular international situation, the extent that he or she can is usually limited.

[7]Considerable historical evidence supports the argument that domestic political concerns were critical for China, Argentina, Egypt, and India. The case is less clear for Iraq, if only bcause less information is available. We feel we know enough at this point to support the view that Iraqi domestic considerations influenced Saddam Hussein's decisionmaking powerfully. Whether they were determinative is not answerable yet.

stability is deemed to be at stake. This case is informed by a number of classic works on this subject and by recently obtained Chinese documents: Mao's Korean War telegrams to Stalin, Chou en Lai, and Chinese military commanders in the field.[8] These data provide a clear picture of Mao's sense of Chinese domestic weakness in the fall of 1950. The Chinese revolution was only two years old at this point; Taiwan was in Nationalist hands; and China was isolated in the world. Her economic situation was dire, and Mao was very concerned that the counterrevolutionary potential in China was dangerously high.

Mao's fears were twofold. First, he was concerned that U.S. and Republic of Korea forces would push into Manchuria and seize China's industrial heartland. However, he was relatively sanguine about this prospect compared to his greater fears that a liberated Korea and a U.S. presence on the Chinese border would imperil the internal order. Such a scenario would have this effect, because it would tie down troops that were needed to menace Taiwan and maintain internal security, be very expensive at a time when China had little cash, and embolden counterrevolutionaries.

Specifically, as Whiting and others have noted, the position of the new Chinese revolutionary regime was quite precarious in 1950. Internal armed resistance had not been entirely suppressed. Large areas in western and southern China remained potentially hostile because of their continued connections to the anticommunist opposition—Kuomintang forces, traditional sources of feudal authority, and non-Chinese ethnic groups. Mao's decision to enter the war was not taken as a crude diversion to the troubled population, although the "diversion" theory may be applicable at times. Rather, he sought to remove an external influence that, if left unrestrained, threatened to amplify critically indigenous sources of instability.

---

[8]See Whiting (1960); Lebow (1981); George and Smoke (1974). In particular, see Christensen (1992), pp. 122–154. This article discusses Chinese decisionmaking in light of recently released Chinese archival materials, including some of Mao's Korean War cables.

Argentina, 1982

Argentina's calculations that led to its attack on the Falklands (Malvinas) illustrate the way war and peace decisions can be crucial to a regime's struggle to retain legitimacy. In this case, Argentina's leaders attempted to buttress their hold on political power through a demonstration of military competence. The reasons they felt compelled to take certain steps illustrate the relationship between internal regime weaknesses and aggressive external behavior.[9]

The military junta in Argentina seized power in March 1976 in response to the incompetence of the Peronistas in managing internal security and the economy. The bloodless coup received widespread popular approval because of the expectation of the military's effectiveness in both of these areas. By early 1982, the junta's incompetence had proved to equal that of the previous regime, and Argentina's middle and upper classes, the military's main supporters, had become disaffected.

During World War II, Argentina had been the most prosperous and advanced state in South America. By 1976, when the junta took power, the Argentine economy had reverted to Third World status because of extensive corruption, national subsidies for various industries and groups, massive public-sector unemployment, and inflation. The junta attempted to rectify this situation through anticorruption and anti-inflation measures and free-market restructuring. Initially, the regime was able to obtain good results, as inflation dropped below 100 percent per year and national growth reached 7 percent in 1979. However, the widespread corruption and other weaknesses of the nation's financial institutions led to the collapse of its leading banks, which produced cascading business failures. By 1981, growth had dropped to less than 1 percent; inflation had reached an annual rate of 150 percent; real wages declined by 18 percent; and unemployment exceeded 15 percent.[10] The junta reacted in the traditional way of authoritarian regimes in this situation: It relaxed the austerity measures, used the public

---

[9]For general information on the Falklands War, see Lebow (1985), pp. 89–124; Hastings and Jenkins (1983); "Falkland Islands—The Origins of a War" (1982), p. 43.

[10]As cited in Lebow (1981), pp. 97–98.

sector to absorb unemployment, and reinstituted government subsidies to prevent the loss of more jobs. Unfortunately, accelerating inflation was the result of the increased money supply needed to maintain these large-scale social programs.

The junta was no more successful in matters of internal security, an area of supposed expertise. In 1976, several left-wing insurgencies were active in Argentina, of which the Montoneros were the best known. The military encouraged the expectation that these groups would be overcome quickly and easily. Instead, what became known as the "Dirty War" ensued, which involved widespread repression, torture, and murder. As many as 20,000 may have been murdered, and many more were arrested or tortured. This "Dirty War" ultimately reached into many of the segments of Argentine society that had supported the 1976 coup.

As a result of its demonstrated incompetence, the junta became increasingly unpopular, especially between 1980 and 1982. Organized labor, which had been badly hurt by the junta's economic policies, staged large protests in major cities in 1982. Farmers and small-business people were openly critical, as well, although they were not well organized. Consistent with the "juggling act" characteristic of authoritarian regimes, the junta mixed repression with a certain measure of increased freedom. As a result, by June 1981, Argentina's five largest political parties joined together in a "common front" to demand open party activity and elections. The junta could not afford simply to deny these demands, and in November 1981 it issued new, freer guidelines for political activity.

Similarly, newspapers became bolder in 1980 and 1981 in their criticisms of the junta. Indeed, *La Prensa* and the *Buenos Aires Herald* openly advocated the reinstitution of civilian national leadership.[11] These and other newspapers also used continuing British sovereignty over the Falklands as illustrative of the junta's shortcomings. When the labor demonstrations reached their peak in March 1982, the junta felt compelled to use the Falklands as a means of reasserting its legitimacy through a demonstration of military competence.

---

[11]As quoted in Lebow (1981), p. 98.

The growing domestic crisis in Argentina dovetailed perfectly with the Conservative electoral victory in Great Britain in 1979. The prior Labor governments of Wilson and Heath had conducted continuous negotiations with Argentina over the sovereignty of the Falklands. Although very slow, these talks had produced movement toward the transfer of sovereignty to Argentina. However, the Thatcher government was much less friendly to this outcome. Negotiations stalled in 1981 and were broken off by the Argentines in early 1982.

Directly after the repudiation of the negotiations on March 3, 1982, the Falklands crisis began when a group of Argentine workmen raised the Argentine flag over South Georgia. They had been landed on the island as part of a long-term contract to remove British scrap metal. It is not clear whether or not the junta knew what the group intended; however, it is clear that Argentine public opinion had been fully aroused over the Falklands by this time. As a result, the junta seized on public approval of the workmen's actions and announced that the Argentine navy would give them "full protection." On March 26, 1982, over 100 Argentine troops landed on South Georgia; on April 2, Argentina invaded the Falklands.

Egypt, 1967

The Arab-Israeli War of 1967 provides another excellent example of the prominent role of regime weakness in the international behavior of Third World states. Specifically, the weakness was a lack of regime legitimacy, leading the Egyptian and Syrian leaderships to undertake risky behavior. In this case, both regimes miscalculated the risks, and war was the result.

A faction of the Ba'thist party seized power from another Ba'thist faction in Syria in February 1966. However, the new regime's stability was quickly threatened by serious factionalism within the governing party, the military, and the larger society. The governing faction attempted to ameliorate these cleavages by reasserting a policy of the forcible elimination of Israel. To this end, the new regime gave active support to Palestinian guerrilla organizations based in Syria and to their cross-border raids into Israel from Syria and Jordan. Tension with Israel grew throughout the summer and fall of 1966. In response, Syria signed a defense pact with Egypt in November 1966. Nasser's claim of Egyptian and personal leadership of the Arab world arose from his vigor in pursuing Arab nationalism and the Palestinian cause. Therefore, to a great extent, he could not separate himself and Egypt from the Israeli-Syrian confrontation without risking dangerous domestic and external criticism.

In the face of increasing casualties inflicted by the *fedayeen* raids, Israel launched a major attack on a Jordanian town, Es Samu, which was a major staging base for Palestinian guerrillas trained in Syria. Egypt did nothing to support Syria and Jordan during the Es Samu operation, in spite of pressure to threaten Israel in the Sinai or to provide Egyptian aircraft to the Jordanians. Nasser justified his inaction by pointing out that the UN Emergency Force (UNEF) formed a buffer in the Sinai between Egyptian and Israeli forces. Syria and Jordan loudly accused Egypt and Nasser of using the UNEF to cover cowardice. In taking this line, Syria and Jordan directly threatened the source of Nasser's legitimacy and, hence, the stability of the Egyptian regime. As a result, Nasser came under strong pressure from his high military commanders to request the withdrawal of the UNEF in December 1966. Nasser resisted this move, believing that the Arabs were unprepared for war.

This uneasy equilibrium of raid and counterraid continued until April 1967, when Syria began shelling Israeli border settlements over disputed claims to the demilitarized zone separating the two states. The artillery exchanges escalated, culminating in a highly public and visible air battle that extended to the outskirts of Damascus. Six Syrian aircraft were destroyed, compared to zero Israeli losses. Again, Egypt took no action, and criticism of Nasser increased. This time, the Egyptians attempted to justify their inaction by asserting that their treaty obligations did not extend to assistance against localized raids. Not surprisingly, Syria and Nasser's domestic opponents dismissed these arguments as evasions. The Soviet Union, concerned about its own interests in Syria, added its weight to the pressures on Nasser to act in some way against Israel.

Matters reached a head in May 1967 when the Soviets notified Egypt that Israel was concentrating forces in preparation for an imminent attack on Syria. The Soviets urged Egypt to deter Israel by deploying large forces into the Sinai. The intention was to signal Israel that a one-front war with Syria was not possible. Such an action had been successful in 1960.[12] As it happened, the Israelis were not concentrating forces against Syria. This reality was reported by the Jordanian and Egyptian intelligence services to their respective governments. However, by this time the Egyptian leadership felt compelled to act or accept possibly fatal damage to its claims to political legitimacy.

On May 14, 1967, the Egyptian army was placed on full alert; some reserves were mobilized; and units on the Suez Canal were ordered to cross into the Sinai. These steps were given great publicity to buttress Nasser's domestic situation and to ensure that the Israelis would receive the signal.[13] On May 16, the Egyptians sent a letter to the commander of the UNEF requesting only its partial withdrawal. Even at this point, Nasser was trying to avoid war with Israel by limiting the provocation he posed. At the same time, he had a competing interest in brinkmanship, to strengthen his political position. He attempted to strike a balance between them. *But, when compelled by events to favor one interest over the other, Nasser saw the risk of war with Israel as preferable to the risks of domestic instability.*

This preference is revealed by what transpired upon receipt of Egypt's May 16 message to the UNEF commander. The request was referred to U Thant, the UN Secretary-General, who informed Egypt that he would consider a request for partial withdrawal equivalent to a demand for complete withdrawal. At this point, Nasser might have been able to use the UN's response for political cover. However, he elected not to take that course. On May 18, Egypt decided "to terminate the presence of UNEF from the territory of the UAR and the Gaza Strip" (Riad, 1981, p. 18). By this action, the greatest obstacle to war had been removed. Israel ordered full-scale mobilization on May 19. Israeli operations against Egypt began on June 5 with well-known results.

---

[12]See Stein (1991), pp. 126–159; Riad (1981); Sadat (1977); Safran (1978). For a somewhat contrary view that recognizes the domestic political pressure on leaders to act, but concludes that deterrence fails only when opportunities to attack arise owing to the lack of credible deterrent threats, see Lieberman (1994).

[13]Ironically, in 1960, the Israelis did not detect the Egyptian advance into the Sinai for almost two days.

In sum, Syria, Jordan, and especially Egypt were captives of domestic fragility. This was a consequence mainly of the discontent of the elite in these countries, although public opinion played a significant role in Egypt and Jordan. Even by May 22, when war with Israel appeared highly likely to the Egyptian leadership, Nasser was described by Sadat as "eager to close the Straits [of Tiran] to maintain his great prestige within the Arab world" (Sadat, 1977, p. 172). Nasser's need to make Egyptian actions public also greatly decreased any flexibility he might have had. Jordan's taunts of Egyptian passivity in 1966 and early 1967 were the result of King Hussein's domestic vulnerability to his Palestinian majority. Indeed, his advisor and cousin, Sharif Zaid Ben Shaker, stated at the end of May 1967 that "If Jordan does not join the war, a civil war will erupt in Jordan."[14] For Syria, public opinion was much less of an issue. The Ba'thists' claim to legitimacy was based on their party's role as a vanguard of secular Arab nationalism. The existence of Israel was always deemed to be inconsistent with that vision, so *any* Ba'thist regime was bound to pursue a policy of eventual confrontation with Israel. However, such a policy did not necessitate a war with Israel in 1967. The reason Israel-Syrian tensions reached the heights they did are directly related to the new Syrian regime's immediate need to play the "Israeli card" as assertively as it could.

India, 1962

The Sino-Indian war in October 1962 provides our last example of the intermingling of domestic stability and international behavior and of how the desire to avert loss (usually loss of political control) leads to increased risk-taking. It also illustrates, as do most of the cases we examine, that a propensity to take high risks is not synonymous with being undeterrable. The Indian leadership was concerned with the military balance with China, and a particular assessment of that balance was crucial in Indian decisionmaking.[15] It follows that, had China been able to alter that particular assessment,

---

[14]Quoted in Stein (1991), p. 142.

[15]See Lebow (1981), pp. 164–169, 184–192; Maxwell (1972); L. Kavic (1967), (1975); Moraes (1956); and Edwardes (1972).

the chances of deterrence success would have been substantially increased.

This war was the result of India's decision to contest Chinese occupation of a disputed border area, the Aksai Chin. The relative equities of the Chinese and Indian claims to the Aksai Chin are irrelevant to this discussion. Interested readers are directed to an extensive literature on the long and rich history of the question (see, for example, Fisher, Rose, and Huttenback, 1963, and Lamb, 1964). Suffice it to say that the dispute had its origins in British colonial decisions over where the Indian border should be drawn. As such, the contest for sovereignty over the Aksai Chin was an outgrowth of one of the many colonial-era negotiations that resulted in troublesome administrative lines drawn on a map.

Following independence in 1947, India asserted its claims to the Aksai Chin. However, a confrontation with China did not occur until the mid-1950s, when India began introducing reconnaissance patrols into the area. These patrols discovered a strategic road that the Chinese had built in the early 1950s to link Sinkiang with Tibet. The discovery became a domestic crisis for Nehru, the Indian Prime Minister and founder of the Congress Party.

Nehru had pursued a consistently friendly policy toward China, even to the point of acquiescence to Chinese occupation of Tibet in 1950. But large and politically weighty elements of the Indian military, the Congress Party, and the foreign policy establishment were quite hostile to China, suspecting it of hegemonic ambitions. Nehru's domination of the Congress Party, indeed of his own cabinet, was partial at best. Many of those who opposed Nehru over his China policy also opposed his broad social and economic reforms. So the border dispute was used to jeopardize Nehru's national domestic objectives; it was used as a proxy for those who had built up a "dislike of Nehru and his charisma, his claim of superiority, his indispensability, his concept of social and economic revolution . . ." (Edwardes, 1972, p. 287). As a result, Nehru had very little room to negotiate a compromise with the Chinese. This became especially true as the Indian population became mobilized over the border dispute in the wake of a sharp firefight between Indian and Chinese troops in August 1959. Nehru is quoted as having told a colleague, "If

I give them that (a negotiated settlement), I shall no longer be Prime Minister of India."[16]

His position was further constrained by a 1960 decision of the Indian Supreme Court, which ruled that any cession of Indian territory required a constitutional amendment. Thus to cede part or all of the Aksai Chin to the Chinese would have required a two-thirds vote in the Parliament plus simple majorities in eight of India's fourteen legislatures, a very difficult process to say the least (Lebow, 1981, p. 188).

In spite of these constraints and pressures, Nehru attempted (as did Nasser in 1966–1967) to walk a balanced course between China and his domestic enemies. To this end, he felt compelled to continue the Indian patrols in the Aksai Chin, although he did not increase them. A second exchange of fire occurred in October 1960. Public opinion reacted with bellicosity toward China. In a speech to the nation, Nehru attempted to rein-in the inflamed Indian sensibilities by taking a moderate line on the shooting. For his pains, he was accused in newspaper editorials of appeasement, weakness, and an "over-scrupulous regard for Chinese susceptibilities and comparative indifference toward the anger and dismay with which the Indian people have reacted."[17]

Nehru never took a conciliatory line again in this matter and responded to this criticism by increasing the Indian presence in the disputed area. A program was begun to construct a network of Indian forward outposts, and deployed Indian forces were ordered to fire on Chinese forces threatening them. A series of clashes ensued, increasing in intensity and cost throughout the remainder of 1961 and 1962. They culminated in a successful Chinese offensive in October 1962, in which China seized the Aksai Chin.

Iraq, 1990

The motivations for Iraq's invasion of Kuwait have been widely debated, primarily over what dominated Saddam Hussein's motiva-

---

[16]Quoted in Lebow (1981), p. 187.
[17]Quoted in Lebow (1981), p. 188.

tions: desire for gain or desire to avert loss (see Stein, 1992, pp. 147–179). While probably not in the desperate domestic straits of Japan in 1941 and North Korea in 1950, many analysts argue that Iraq's situation contained important parallels. This may explain some of Iraq's willingness to accept risks that surprised Western observers during the Gulf crisis of 1990–1991.

From 1980 through 1989, Iraq incurred $80 billion in foreign debt, mostly to sustain its war with Iran. About 50 percent was owed to Arab states, especially Saudi Arabia, Kuwait, and the United Arab Emirates (UAE).[18] By 1990, Iraq's creditors had become extremely concerned over Iraq's ability to meet its debt-servicing schedules. As a result, additional credit became difficult for Saddam to obtain.

The nub of his problem was financing national reconstruction after the ruinous war with Iran. Estimates of the cost of reconstruction were in excess of $230 billion. Yet the national budget of Iraq was already running a deficit of about $10 billion per year just to maintain the status quo. Obviously, the additional burden of reconstruction was unaffordable without new sources of capital. In principle, this could be obtained from three sources. First, the existing debt could be forgiven or rescheduled. Forgiveness was rejected by the creditors, and rescheduling could provide only small relief. Second, new credit could be extended, but that too was rejected by the creditors. Finally, Iraq could obtain hard currency from increased revenues from oil sales. Unfortunately, a higher oil price was needed. In the late 1980s, the price of oil had begun to fall, a trend that was still under way in early 1990. Iraq's attempt to arrest this slide by lowering production quotas was rejected by Kuwait and the UAE, the two biggest violators of the existing Organization of Petroleum Exporting Countries (OPEC) quota. By the beginning of 1990, OPEC was exceeding its production quota by 2 million barrels per day, with Kuwait and the UAE accounting for 75 percent of the surplus.[19]

Beginning at the Arab Cooperation Council summit in February 1990, the Iraqis began an intense diplomatic effort to induce or co-

---

[18]See, for example, Davis and Arquilla (1991b); Freedman and Karsh (1993), pp. 37–38; Karsh and Rautsi (1991), pp. 18–30; Gross (1992), pp. 147–179.

[19]At that time, OPEC's production quota was 22 million barrels per day. Actual production was 24 million barrels per day.

erce Kuwait and the UAE to agree to lower quotas, reduce their own production, and forgive Iraq's wartime debts. Kuwait and the UAE remained indifferent to Iraq's pleas and threats. By mid-July 1990, Iraq had begun its military buildup opposite Kuwait.

The important deterrence question is to what extent Iraq's debt situation and lack of additional credit imperiled Saddam Hussein's regime—or, at least, that this was believed by the Iraqi leadership. To the extent the regime was endangered, Saddam's decisionmaking could be said to be motivated by a desire to avert loss, i.e., his hold on power. Decisionmakers in this predicament have a propensity to accept high risks and so are hard to deter. To the extent the regime was not imperiled, Saddam's decisionmaking could be said to be motivated by desire for gain, i.e., Kuwait's vulnerable oil riches. Such decisionmakers most often are chary of risk and easier to deter. Certainly at the time of the crisis, the prevailing view in the United States was that Saddam was motivated primarily by the latter rather than the former. This presumption may explain some of the continuing surprise at Saddam's stubbornness in trying to hold Kuwait in the face of such overwhelming force. Many observers felt that the Iraqis would surely retreat from Kuwait at the last moment under the cover of Russian or French mediation. Of course, this did not happen, a pattern of behavior more consistent with a desire to avert loss than purely a matter of gain. For this reason, a number of analysts of the Gulf War take the view that Saddam's "political survival and his long-term ambitions" hinged on the national reconstruction that could not be undertaken without some debt relief.[20] If so, Iraq would have been difficult to deter from invading Kuwait (though probably not impossible) and even more difficult to compel to leave. So it proved. Beyond this, we cannot go without better information.

DETERRABILITY OF REGIONAL ADVERSARIES

Thus far, the discussion has illustrated the vulnerability of some regional adversaries to domestic pressures to act internationally and the ways those pressures can result in acceptance of high risks. By

---

[20]See Stein (1992); Freedman and Karsh (1993); and Karsh and Rautsi (1991). For an opposing view, see Mylroie (1993).

definition, a willingness to accept risks suggests that deterrence of such regimes is difficult. Indeed, it proved so in the cases cited here.

However, these and other cases also suggest strongly that deterrence is not *impossible* in these situations, although it may be difficult and effortful. Specifically, virtually every case we studied in detail suggested (sometimes explicitly, sometimes indirectly) that Third World regimes are deterrable in such crises. The evidence for this is contained in the memoirs of the participants, primary source materials arising from meetings, and strategic instructions formulated to provide guidance for commanders and civilian decisionmakers. We again turn to the cases of China in 1950, Argentina in 1982, Egypt in 1967, India in 1962, and Iraq in 1990 to illustrate these points.[21]

HISTORICAL EVIDENCE THAT DETERRENCE WAS POSSIBLE

China, 1950

With stakes as high as regime preservation, one would predict that China would have been very difficult to deter. In fact, that seems to have been true. Mao recognized clearly the risk the United States could pose of striking urban-industrial targets from the air with conventional and *nuclear* weapons. China, after all, had no means to respond directly to this threat. Ironically, this threat led Mao to take the most aggressive course he could. He reasoned that the presence of U.S. forces anywhere in Korea posed an unacceptable risk to Chinese domestic arrangements. A Chinese offensive to drive the United States merely below the 38th parallel would be unsatisfactory. The United States still would be left in possession of Korean bases from which it could wage a strategic air war against China. Indeed, Mao's worst-case scenario was a stalemate on the Korean peninsula leaving the U.S. free and motivated to undertake strategic bombardment of China from within easy range. Therefore, Mao elected to commit forces sufficient to drive the United States entirely off the peninsula in one blow as quickly as possible. In that way, the U.S.

---

[21]One of the classic examples of a very risk-acceptant regime that was still deterrable is Japan's in its deliberations about war in the summer of 1941. Japan was not a Third World adversary, so that case has not been included in the body of the text. However, since it is still interesting and instructive, it has been included in Appendix B.

capability to strike Chinese targets could be reduced to a "more tolerable scope and duration."

This case is a good example of the domination of the costs of inaction over the risks of all other courses, at least in the eyes of the Chinese leadership. The presence of U.S. forces north of the 38th parallel was deemed a mortal threat, so to do nothing was unacceptable as soon as the U.S. forces crossed the 38th parallel. Mao stated this explicitly in his wires to Marshall Peng Duhai and Stalin. Apparently, no buffer arrangement with the United States along the Yalu would have ameliorated his fears. Therefore, Chinese strategic decisionmaking shifted to evaluating ways in which the benefits of an inevitable and risky war could be maximized. In that process, Mao accepted the possibility that China could be struck severe blows. There is no evidence in his telegrams of confidence that the Soviets would or could deter the United States from attacking China. Thus, Mao deemed nuclear bombardment of Chinese cities less risky than tolerating U.S. forces on China's border.

Seen in this light, the prospects for deterring the Chinese were substantially reduced after the 38th parallel was crossed. This resolves the question posed by Thomas Schelling as to why the Chinese prepared their attack in secret, and launched it by surprise, if their objective was to deter the United States from crossing the Yalu (Christensen, 1992, p. 141). In Mao's view, deterrence of the United States had failed much earlier and, accordingly, deterrence of Chinese intervention became extremely difficult—but, perhaps, not impossible.

Mao's Korean War telegrams provide evidence that, as motivated as the Chinese were, they were not nondeterrable (Christensen, 1992, pp. 137–140). In the telegrams, Mao discusses his worst-case scenario: a failure to eject the U.S. forces from the Korean peninsula, followed by prolonged stalemate and U.S. bombardment of the mainland. It follows logically that Mao's strategic calculations might well have been affected *if the United States had been able to pose a credible threat that a Chinese attack would have resulted in Mao's worst case.* Presumably, this would have required the United States to establish a declaratory policy of this intention, and to reinforce and configure its advancing forces in Korea to make them clearly capable of resisting a Chinese attack. Ground forces would have been necessary for this task, since the Chinese had assessed correctly that the air forces of that period could not halt a Chinese offensive with the coalition's ground forces deployed as they were.

Argentina, 1982

Could Argentina have been deterred by the British? Approximately one month passed between Argentina's first hostile action (support for the workers on South Georgia) and the full-blown invasion of the Falklands. During that period, the British were cautious to the point of passivity. As is so often the case, the problem the British government faced was ambiguous intelligence, a strong predisposition to believe that the Argentines would not act "irrationally," and a classic concern that aggressive British action would provoke rather than deter.[22] This is not the place to assess British policy. Rather, the question is whether Argentina could have been deterred from invading the Falklands after the South Georgia event. Obviously, this question is impossible to answer, but several general points can be made.

The junta did not believe itself to be in control of events. This sense of compulsion is typical of a regime that deems its stability to be at stake. Endangered regimes usually believe they have no other choice but to take a desperate course of action. However, they seldom choose a course of action that they understand at the time to be virtually certain to fail.[23] Therefore, could the British have presented the Argentines with that prospect?

The British chose the most difficult option, which was to execute an amphibious landing and a subsequent ground campaign. There is good evidence that Argentina's planners thought that the British prospects of success in this endeavor were small and that the British themselves shared that assessment. In Argentina's view, once Argentine troops (regardless of their poor preparation) reached the

---

[22]See Jervis (1976) for a discussion of the "spiral" model. The spiral model describes the conditions in which threats intended to be inhibiting are actually stimulating to an adversary.

[23]As we said, the exceptions to this generalization are states in such dire straits that literally any alternative is preferred to doing nothing. But such states are rare.

Falklands, the British would be compelled to negotiate. Thus, as long as the Argentines felt certain that they could deploy a force into the Falklands, they could not be deterred by the British threat to expel them.

However, the British had the naval capability to have greatly increased the risks to Argentina's troop deployments, the bulk of which were moved by ships. The British could have used attack submarines to isolate the Falklands from the mainland. Indeed, David Owen made exactly this point (Stein, 1992, p. 109). It would have been possible to implement this policy if one or two submarines had been dispatched to the South Atlantic at the time of the South Georgia incident. Also, tactical aircraft or surface-to-air missiles could have been deployed to the Falklands airstrip to prevent Argentina from airlifting troops instead of sealifting them. Though Argentina might have contemplated contesting air superiority over the Falklands, it would have been helpless to contest control of the sea—a reality its leaders understood fully. Therefore, there are good reasons to suppose that the announcement that British submarines would prevent reinforcement of the Falklands would have been an effective deterrent, especially if coupled with an offer to renew negotiations over sovereignty. No doubt, the Argentines might have tested the British to ensure against a bluff. The British submarines could have given a graphic demonstration of their capabilities, and Argentina would have been entirely helpless to rectify their situation. Indeed, when H.M.S. *Conqueror* sank the *General Belgrano* on May 3, Argentina's surface navy never ventured again into the theater of operations.

One can debate whether the threat should have been made publicly or privately. Certainly, one characteristic of submarines is that they can be covertly deployed, thus making it possible to keep threats private. This threat, public or private, would have confronted the junta with a virtually assured risk of failure. Unless the junta believed its chances of political survival to be even less likely, or it simply disbelieved the British threat, it likely would have been deterred by such a British move.

Egypt, 1967

Could the Egyptians have been deterred from pursuing confrontation, especially in May 1967? As with the cases of China and

Argentina, there is evidence that Nasser could have been deterred. Although highly motivated by political considerations, Nasser devoted considerable attention to the question of the military balance between the two sides. His closest associates suggest that he would not have continued to escalate had he not concluded that Israel was militarily inferior (see Safran, 1978, pp. 397–398).

One reason for his misimpression was the Egyptian-Syrian defense agreement, which placed Syrian forces under Egyptian command. In May 1967, Jordan agreed to do the same, and arrangements were made to bring Egyptian and Iraqi troops into Jordan. The result was to compel Israel to fight a three-front war, its worst case. Nasser was undeterred by Israel *not* because he doubted Israel's resolve, but because he doubted Israel's capability. He did assess military balances, even in the midst of intense crisis, and that assessment was instrumental in his decision to go forward. Therefore, the Israelis should have been able to affect that decision, if they could have altered Nasser's view of the military balance. Thus Nasser was deterrable. Indeed, as was true with the Chinese in 1950, despite great differences in culture, values, and political system, the Egyptians and Israelis spoke a common deterrence language, albeit unsuccessfully.

India, 1962

Why did the Chinese fail in their attempts to deter the Indians? As with the other cases, the Indian leadership believed that its domestic political position was weak and that demonstrations of external "strength" could ameliorate that condition. Such behavior can be imperfectly analogized to "overcompensation" in psychodynamic theory. An individual may respond to weakness in one area by hyperaggressiveness and rigidity in another. Such behavior is not the exclusive province of Third World leaders. But Third World regimes tend to be fragile, so events that might be difficult for any leader become "life threatening" for them. Therefore, Nehru and India plainly fall into the "hard-to-deter" category. But "hard to deter" does not mean "impossible to deter."

We make this point because of the strong evidence that Nehru was very interested in the Sino-Indian military balance. Specifically, he had quite an optimistic (although misguided) view of the capabilities of the Indian forces to defeat the Chinese (Maxwell, 1972, pp. 240–

242). The fact that such an assessment was unrealistic misses the point that consideration of the balance was central to Nehru's risk-taking behavior. Further, his view was widely shared, even among Indians alarmed by the aggressiveness of Nehru's actions. It follows that the Chinese might have deterred the Indians had they found a way to communicate effectively their actual capabilities. Chinese caution prior to their October attack reportedly was taken by the Indians as evidence of the correctness of the Indian assessment.[24]

Iraq, 1990

The deterrability of Iraq in 1990 is the most difficult to discuss because of the dearth of direct information that has proven so valuable in the other cases. Instead, we need to rely primarily on two well-done analyses of this question (Davis and Arquilla, 1991b, and Stein, 1992, pp. 147–179).

Both studies interestingly focus on what we would agree is the central question: Saddam Hussein's motivations. Was he an "opportunity-driven aggressor or a vulnerable leader motivated by need" (Stein, 1992, p. 155)?

Davis and Arquilla describe this as Model One and Model Two. Model One corresponds roughly to the "vulnerable leader motivated by need" and Model Two to the "opportunity-driven aggressor" (Davis and Arquilla, 1991b, pp. 12–15).

Both studies conclude that Saddam Hussein probably could have been deterred from invading Kuwait, regardless of which motivation dominated his calculations. Stein notes particularly the usefulness of combining deterrence threats with promises of rewards for desirable behavior. In the case of Iraq, that reward would have taken the form of debt relief.

Davis and Arquilla are more specific in their conclusions. They argue that a U.S. preinvasion tripwire force in Kuwait "might well have de-

---

[24]Note the parallel between the effects of caution in this case and those in the Falklands invasion. It suggests that the period following the first provocation by the aggressor is especially important for communicating credible deterrence. Passivity at this point can be very dangerous.

terred his (Hussein's) invasion" (Davis and Arquilla, 1991b, p. 69). They also emphasize the importance of early action before the adversary has committed himself and before the problem becomes one of compellence rather than deterrence.

CONCLUSIONS

In sum, these cases show how states that believe that very risky international action will avert a domestic crisis will be hard to deter from that action. Unfortunately, many regional adversaries fall into this category; however, such adversaries usually are not impossible to deter. But deterrence is likely to be difficult, expensive, effortful, and dependent on accurate information about how the adversary evaluates his situation.

The cases suggest that successful deterrence would have been possible if the adversary could have been persuaded to a high degree of certainty that he could not achieve his military objectives and that efforts to do so would leave him in a dangerously poorer status quo. The primary criteria that these regional regimes used in determining the likelihood of their success were *military.* Could the objectives be achieved against the military defenses likely to be encountered? If the answer was thought to be "no" to that question, the evidence supports the view that the attackers would not have initiated the conflicts. In spite of the strength of the domestic needs—the costs of inaction—none of the regimes we examined was prepared to commit national suicide. They all had a theory of victory by which their military forces would succeed, and in no case were those theories irrational or crazy—although they involved high risks.

The implication of this reasoning is that such adversaries are deterrable by military measures that convincingly invalidate the adversary's theory of victory. Obviously, deterrence in these instances is narrow and limited. The hostile intentions of the adversary are left unchanged. Only the specific military action has been deterred, leaving the situation unchanged and the adversary likely to try again tomorrow. However, this sort of deterrence success is no small thing and, in any case, is all that can be reasonably expected of deterrence. Deterrence, in a sense, is a superficial policy, for it cannot affect the roots of the problem; it can only stifle it. Nevertheless, in a world of flawed and crude instruments, that may be the best one can do.

Thus far, we have tried to build a case that many regional adversaries are hard but not impossible to deter. Further, even with highly motivated adversaries, military forces are an effective instrument for making a deterrent threat if they can be tailored to persuade the adversary that his theory of victory cannot succeed. The following questions now arise:

- How can such threats be made credibly to regional adversaries?
- What military forces are especially useful as deterrents?

Chapter Four addresses the first question, Chapter Five the second.

THE CREDIBILITY OF U.S. DETERRENT THREATS

Credibility has two facets. The first is whether the adversary believes the United States *intends* to do what it threatens to do. This usually is a function of the strength of the U.S. interests the adversary deems to be at stake. Note also that it is really *future* U.S. intention that is the issue here: Will the United States try to implement its threat at the time in the future when deterrence is tested? The second is whether the adversary believes the United States is *capable* of doing what it threatens. This is a function of the adversary's assessment of the military balance with the United States. Overall credibility is, in a sense, the product of these separate elements, intent and capability. If the future intention is gauged to be zero and if capability is immense, the overall credibility is zero. Similarly, all the intent in the world cannot make threats credible if there is no capability to carry them out. However, between these extremes, the communication of a strong will to act can compensate to some extent for a less certain military capability. Similarly, a fearsome military capability can compensate for some uncertainty the adversary may feel about the U.S. will to act. This, after all, was the foundation of nuclear deterrence, especially in the context of NATO.[1]

This chapter is devoted to a discussion of the first of the two aspects of credibility: communicating intent. The following chapter on mili-

---

[1] Empirical investigation of intent and capability confirms that both matter in decisionmaking and that an overabundance of one can compensate for too little of the other—within limits. This point is born out specifically in the deterrence literature. See, for example, Huth (1988).

tary capabilities touches on the problem of credibly communicating U.S. capabilities for doing what it threatens to do.

There are two principal facets of intent: interests and reputation. At least one, and preferably both, must be robust for the intention to carry out a threat to be credible. If a state has very substantial interests in another state, it is more likely to commit itself to the other's defense. Therefore, to make commitments believable, a state has to behave as though its interests are engaged. Generally, this means establishing various types of ties and arrangements with the state to be defended. These include such things as political and economic relationships, formal defense arrangements, and the deployment or frequent presence of forces overseas.

Collectively, these measures can be called indicators of a state's interests. By these measures, U.S. interests in Europe and South Korea are quite high, as reflected by the extensive political, economic, and military ties; the existence of formal alliances; and the fact that these ties have withstood the test of time. On the other hand, U.S. ties to Bosnia or Somalia are weak or nonexistent. This, combined with erratic statements by U.S. leaders, suggests that U.S. interests in these regions are low.

Considerable qualitative and quantitative evidence bears out the relationship between the existence of ties and deterrence success. Indeed, scrutiny of the aggregate data derived from a large number of historical cases suggests that perception of interests is at least as weighty a variable as comparative military capabilities in explaining when deterrence will succeed or fail.[2]

Reputation refers to a state's record of past behavior. To a certain extent, reputation can substitute for a clear perception of interests. Reputation is established by previous actions and may reflect a leader's propensity for doing what he says, a leader's predispositions (e.g., a preference for negotiated settlements), a state's past behavior with respect to certain interests, or the military's capability for conducting certain types of operations successfully or unsuccessfully.

---

[2]Jervis (1976); Jervis, Lebow, and Stein (1985); George and Smoke (1974); Huth and Russett (1984), pp. 496, 526.

Although concerns for reputation seem to exert great pressure on decisionmakers, it is a relatively uninvestigated area in both the academic and policy-analytic literature. The historical case studies we used were not particularly helpful in shedding light on the importance or fragility of reputation as a factor in explaining deterrence success or failure. The best work in this area has been done by Paul Huth, Bruce Russett, Jonathan Shimshoni, and Elli Lieberman.[3] Their results suggest that reputation can be important, in addition to interests, in buttressing credibility. However, all four find that reputation can be quite limited in its effects. For example, a state's reputation for behavior seems to be specific to the events that created that reputation. This suggests that U.S. credibility in Europe probably was not damaged a great deal by difficulties in Vietnam. But, on the other hand, U.S. success in the recent Gulf War probably has little positive effect on U.S. credibility in Bosnia.

One of the more troubling reputations the United States has acquired is for heightened sensitivity to casualties. Many foreign, as well as American, leaders believe that U.S. public opinion will turn against any conflict or war as soon as U.S. casualties begin to mount, leading the public to demand withdrawal. This sensitivity implies that U.S. threats to intervene are less credible if the adversary believes he can inflict sufficient casualties on U.S. forces, where the word "sufficient" is intended to suggest some match between the level of casualties and American perceptions of the interest at stake.

Our research suggests that there is a fundamental flaw in this perception. While it is true that U.S. public approval for conflicts drops as casualties mount, this decreased public approval should not be equated with a public desire to withdraw. *Rather, polling evidence from Korea, Vietnam, and the war with Iraq suggests that public disapproval is almost always associated with a public desire to end the conflict more quickly and cheaply by escalation, if that would be effective.* Rather than cutting U.S. losses by withdrawing, the public reaction is as often to cut U.S. losses by "taking the gloves off." Eventually, if it becomes clear that the United States will not escalate, the U.S. public will increasingly press for withdrawal as the only way to end pointless casualties. Note this explanation of U.S. casualty

---

[3]See Huth (1988), Huth and Russett (1988), Shimshoni (1988), and Lieberman (1994).

sensitivity is very different from the cliché that the U.S. simply has no "stomach" for casualties. The implications for regional deterrence are important. Regional leaders might have a very different image of U.S. resolve if they understood the real content of U.S. public opinion.[4]

Besides interests and reputation, two lesser factors—bargaining tactics and perceptions of legitimacy—also influence the perception of a state's resolve to act in defense of some interest. To some extent, these factors simply amplify the perception of interests and reputation discussed above. However, they also can be quite distinct. Hence, they are mentioned separately.

Thomas Schelling was the first to articulate a long list of bargaining tactics important for deterrence (see Schelling, 1966, Ch 2). Among them are the "rationality of irrationality," i.e., convincing an opponent that a threat will be carried out even if it hurts the defender (this could be an aspect of the leadership's reputation); convincing an opponent that he has the "last clear chance" to avoid the confrontation (i.e., relinquishing control over events, for example, by making retaliation automatic if the proscribed action occurs); and clear public declarations of one's intent to defend an ally, which makes it hard to back down from the commitment without incurring some damage to one's reputation (i.e., tying one's hands to some extent). The extent to which some of these tactics can be effectively employed by the leaders of a state is debatable. Nevertheless, one should at least be aware that bargaining tactics can affect the perception of credibility.

The perceived legitimacy of the defender's interests, or of his methods of defense, is more difficult to determine.[5] Nevertheless, if the challenger believes the defender's claim to some interest is legitimate, or that his own claim is less legitimate, then the challenger is likely to believe the defender has greater resolve in defending that

---

[4]Public opinion polls taken during the Korean and Vietnam Wars show that Americans do grow weary of protracted wars as casualties mount. However, these same polls show that Americans do not wish to withdraw from the conflict. Rather, casualties lead to a growing desire to escalate the conflict in an effort to resolve it more quickly. See Schwarz (1994).

[5]For a discussion of the concept of legitimacy and its influence on international behavior, see Bull (1977), although the use of the concept of legitimacy in this report is somewhat different from Bull's.

claim. For example, major powers frequently believe the existing international system is legitimate. The challenger may not share this belief. However, if the challenger understands that major powers believe this to be true, the challenger is likely to believe they will have greater resolve to uphold the status quo. Note that this does not require the challenger to agree with the legitimacy of the defender's claim, only that he believe the defender believes this. Frequently, crisis diplomacy is designed to increase international perceptions of the legitimacy of one side's cause in a conflict and to decrease the perception of the opponent's legitimacy. Attempts to label the opponent as the "aggressor" and oneself as the "defender" in a crisis are an obvious example, or attempts by leaders to seek justifications for their actions in internal law.

The notion of legitimacy can also be applied to the methods used to defend interests. Certain types of weapons (e.g., chemical and biological weapons), or certain types of warfare (e.g., terrorism) may be perceived by the international community to be illegitimate for advancing a state's interests. To the extent this is true, threats to use these weapons will not be perceived to be legitimate. For example, if the international community believes that terrorism is not a legitimate means for addressing grievances, a state that threatens terrorist acts will have more difficulty convincing the defender of its resolve, since the defender may dismiss such threats as illegitimate. Put another way, the challenger, knowing that the defender believes terrorism to be illegitimate, will likely believe the defender's resolve to deter such threats, if only because the defender will have greater international sympathy for making strong counterthreats. Again, note that the challenger does not have to agree with the defender's perspective that certain means are not legitimate. All that is required is that the challenger believe the defender holds this belief.

Thus, the utility of establishing international norms against the use of certain weapons or types of warfare is not to convince the world of the rectitude of one's moral stance, but rather the pragmatic utility of undermining the coercive power of such threats.

Focusing on U.S. interests and reputation, one can draw several implications for regional deterrence. First, committing oneself to defending a particular interest is an effective way to communicate the intent to act, and, as such, commitments are an important deterrence tool. But, by definition, U.S. commitments must be few and selective, because real commitments are costly. Rhetorical commitments given promiscuously are not only incredible but may diminish the credibility of more serious commitments. Moreover, commitments cannot be created at the *time of a crisis*. Time is needed to develop a network of political, economic, and military ties with an endangered state. This means that the most credible commitment is one established well before the crisis and continually reinforced by tangible actions. Signals of commitment at the time of crisis may be useful to *remind* an adversary of an existing commitment, but they cannot establish that commitment in the absence of a historical record. Unfortunately, commitment is often an unreliable source of credibility for the United States, because, as a global power, the United States often seeks to exercise deterrence in regions where it has few past commitments. Also, the United States often does not know what its interests are until they are endangered. The classic example is Korea in 1950. It took the actual experience of an invasion to make U.S. interests salient enough to spur action.

This problem of "revealed interests" makes it difficult for the United States to establish commitments of various kinds to all the states on whose behalf it might act. Therefore, the United States often finds itself trying to assert a commitment in the absence of a believable record of action.[6] This also means that the Flexible Deterrence Options in the U.S. National Military Strategy are unlikely to be effective signals of intent in cases in which there has been no discernible record of a strong U.S. interest.[7] They are much more likely to be effective in crises in which evidence of U.S. interest is apparent.

Second, reputation can compensate for some of these difficulties with commitment. But reputation, by definition, depends upon a

---

[6]Bosnia is a good example. The Balkans have not been an area to which the United States has committed itself in the past.

[7]Flexible Deterrence Options are military actions a theater commander can take in the early days of a crisis to signal a potential adversary that the United States is committed to the defense of its threatened interests. Such actions might be the movement of a carrier battle group to a position more conducive to air strikes. Usually, the forces immediately at hand to a commander-in-chief for Flexible Deterrence Options are not sufficient to deny the adversary his objectives. Rather, the hope is that the early, forcible expression of U.S. commitment will deter the adversary from taking further steps.

record of action and, hence, cannot be created at the time of a crisis. Moreover, evaluation of historical case studies suggests that the power of reputation to enhance credibility is limited (see Shimshoni, 1988, pp. 231–234). Reputation appears to be specific to a given adversary or region and is not readily generalized. In this sense, the United States has multiple reputations, each connected to different situations.

Reputation also probably has an unfortunately short half-life. Even for situations similar to the war with Iraq, the U.S. reputation is unlikely to last for a decade without "booster shots" from other successful military interventions. Thus, the euphoric expectation that Operation Desert Storm would be some sort of anodyne for U.S. credibility is based on an illusion about the durability of reputation.

There is little that can be done about these problems of commitment and reputation. The United States can make clear commitments only to a limited number of states or regions, for example, Western Europe, Israel, Saudi Arabia and the Persian Gulf, Japan, and Korea. The credibility of U.S. deterrent threats extended to these interests is likely to be high. Elsewhere in the world, U.S. credibility is less assured, and one must expect that deterrence there will be more difficult. As mentioned earlier, there frequently are good reasons for resisting commitments to many areas. Commitments bolster credibility by binding a state to courses of action it later may wish to avoid. Violating a commitment damages reputation; inaction in the absence of a commitment is probably less damaging.

Therefore, the United States simply will have to live with the tensions of having global interests, but only a limited number of vital ones that warrant a clear commitment. Nevertheless, the United States may want to deter threats to U.S. interests not covered by a prior commitment. Reputation may be a substitute but only in a limited way. Military capability may be able to make up for these deficiencies in commitment and reputation. That is, U.S. regional deterrence strategy should probably rely more on convincing potential adversaries that the United States can respond overwhelmingly if it so chooses, rather than on convincing them that U.S. willingness to intervene is high. The latter may simply be too difficult in cases in which U.S. vital interests are not clearly engaged. The discussion of what military capabilities would be useful in this regard is taken up in the next chapter.

Chapter Five

THE MILITARY DIMENSIONS OF DETERRENCE

It seems odd that small regional powers would ever challenge the United States, or any other great power for that matter. Yet, this occurs quite frequently. Argentina went to war with Great Britain over the Falkland Islands; Libya intervened in the Chadian civil war in the early 1980s despite threats from France; and Iraq attacked Kuwait despite warnings from the United States. One explanation, of course, is that regional powers do not believe the major power will respond. If so, the military balance is less relevant. However, even when credible deterrent threats appear to be made, many regional powers still choose war (see Wolf, 1991, and Arquilla, 1992).

Some commentators have suggested that regional powers ignore military factors in their decisions about whether or not to go to war. This explanation is not compelling, because it suggests highly irrational or impulsive behavior on the part of leaders in situations that could lead to the loss of their regime, if not their entire country. While such irrationality is not impossible, the historical evidence suggests that it is quite rare. The relative roles and weights of military and nonmilitary factors in explaining the success or failure of deterrence remain among the most unsettled issues in the deterrence literature. Those who argue against the importance of military factors do so on the basis of what might be called a "push" theory of deterrence. That is, they argue that states are impelled or pushed irresistibly into international crises for reasons of necessity. If "forced" by necessity to take risks, states must largely forgo the rational calculation of costs and benefits, which are so much a part of classical deterrence theory. As a consequence, military balance assessment ought to be of little import in crisis decisionmaking. Note that this style of argument is quite similar to what we have described as the state that "has nothing to lose," discussed earlier. These states occupy the extreme left side of the deterrence continuum portrayed in Figure 2.

On the basis of the cases examined, we find that the proponents of this "push" theory of deterrence overstate the prevalence of states with so little to lose that they cease to be interested in the risks attendant to their actions. Certainly, as illustrated by the cases of Japan, North Korea, and Cuba, there are states with little or nothing to lose. For such states, the military balance probably is secondary in their calculations. Certainly, regional adversaries frequently feel powerfully the push of domestic exigencies to engage in international risk-taking, and this can make them hard to deter. But few regional adversaries feel the push so strongly as to render the relative military balance irrelevant. Indeed, we have found that the military balance powerfully shapes behavior in the great majority of deterrence situations, even when the adversaries are separated by great gulfs in values, objectives, history, and political systems. Recall the cases discussed in Chapter Three on the character and motivations of regional states. In each of these cases, we found specific evidence that decisionmakers paid close attention to the relevant military balance. It is true that their perceptions of the balances were often flawed, but that is hardly unusual and, in any case, is not the point. The point is that the military balance was a central feature in the calculations of decisionmakers. Indeed, as discussed in those cases, it is possible to deduce from the historical record what it likely would have taken to have deterred the attackers. Therefore, while we obviously believe the push model of international crises, as advanced by Lebow, Jervis, and Stein, has much merit, we find that they go much further than the data will bear, presumably in the interests of distinguishing themselves as much as possible from more traditional formulations of deterrence.

The perspective advanced here is that regional leaders do take the relative military balance into account when deciding whether or not to use military force to accomplish their objectives. However, not all dimensions of military power are equally important. Otherwise, regional states would never challenge great-power interests. The question is, which military factors are most salient?

THE LOCAL MILITARY BALANCE

Regional powers seek quick, decisive military results, not long wars of attrition.[1] While this is true for major powers as well, there are several factors that make it particularly true for Third World states. First, the financial and military costs of such wars are often ruinous for small states. Many of these states cannot maintain conflicts for extended periods without severely sapping their economic strength.[2] Second, long wars exacerbate domestic political instabilities and frequently unleash political forces that can topple the regime. In contrast, rapidly achieved victories may be quite popular. The difference with democratic states is that, although long wars may topple the current administration, the democratic political systems are not so vulnerable as to collapse.[3] For many regional powers, the collapse of the current political regime brings with it the downfall of much of the bureaucratic structure. In short, long wars can be politically and economically disastrous for regional states.

If short wars are the basis for planning, it is logical that the military capabilities that can deny regional leaders a quick victory will likely have the greatest deterrent influence.[4] With respect to extended deterrence, regional adversaries may decide to attack another state if they believe they can accomplish their objectives so quickly that they present the defender with a *fait accompli* before the defender can meaningfully come to the aid of its ally. The gamble is that the de-

---

[1]Many analysts and scholars have noted this point. See, for example, Mearsheimer (1983) and Anderson and McKeown (1997), pp. 17–22. Notable exceptions to this might be revolutionary governments, such as North Vietnam's under Ho Chi Minh, who chose low-level guerrilla warfare tactics when facing a more advanced military opponent, because guerrilla warfare played to their strengths.

[2]For example, Saddam Hussein suffered serious economic problems in the wake of his 8-year war with Iran (1980–1988), as did Vietnam in its struggle to defeat the United States.

[3]Certainly, democratic political leaders can be and have been voted out of office, even in the midst of war. But these changes of leadership do not result in the end of the political system.

[4]This turns out to be a surprisingly contentious point. For arguments emphasizing the importance of military factors in deterrence failure or success, see Huth and Russett (1984); Huth (1988); Huth and Russett (1988), pp. 29–45; Huth and Russet (1990), pp. 466–501; Huth and Russett (1993); and George and Smoke (1974). For arguments that military factors are secondary, see Stein (1987), pp. 326–352; Maoz, (1983), pp. 195–230; Levy (1988).

fender will not attempt to roll back the attacker at some later time, because the effort involved and the potential costs will be too great.[5]

That said, what aspects of the military balance are most important for deterrence? If denying the adversary a quick, cheap victory is most important, the military capabilities that can perform that task are most relevant for deterrence. The allied and U.S. forces in theater, or the forces that can be deployed to the theater in a short period of time, should weigh most heavily on a regional leader's mind. Slower-deploying forces (e.g., most active and reserve forces in the continental United States) are less likely to deter the adversary, although such forces make an important contribution to U.S. warfighting capabilities.[6]

Local or early-arriving forces and later-arriving forces both may be highly effective warfighting tools. Each may be equally able to defeat an adversary. Indeed, since later-arriving ground forces often consist of heavy armored forces, they may be more effective from the warfighting point of view. The problem is that these two types of forces are not usually equal in their deterrence power. Adversaries are more likely to find it credible that they will actually have to contend with local or early-arriving forces if they challenge U.S. deterrence, because later-arriving forces require great effort, expense, and time to deploy. Moreover, they arrive after the opponent has consolidated his hold over his military objective, thus presenting the defender with a more difficult military obstacle. In short, they are easy to discount. Therefore, in the absence of especially strong reasons to believe the United States will actually deploy its later-arriving forces,

---

[5]For example, in 1950, the North Korean regime believed that if it could rapidly defeat South Korean forces and sweep the small U.S. contingent off the peninsula, the United States would not have the political will to reinvade the peninsula to roll back the North Koreans to the 38th Parallel. Similar thinking affected Japanese decisionmaking, leading to the attack on Pearl Harbor. Saddam Hussein may have believed that if he conquered Kuwait quickly, the United States would not expend the effort to roll back Iraq, especially if this military operation appeared costly in terms of casualties. Saddam Hussein certainly tried to convince the United States that uprooting Iraqi troops dug in along the Kuwait-Saudi border would inflict a large number of casualties. Even after the air war started, Saddam Hussein held to his view that the inevitable ground war would be costly and, hence, that the United States could not forcibly eject him from Kuwait.

[6]This observation has been made by many. The numerous studies cited earlier by Huth and Russett arrive at similar conclusions. So too does Arquilla (1991).

adversaries find local and early-arriving forces more credible and germane to their assessments of the military balance.

A furthur distinction can be made between local forces forward deployed and early-arriving forces, because early-arriving forces still require a political decision to deploy. If an adversary believes the political will to commit such forces is lacking, early-arriving forces would be less effective as a deterrent than local forces. Put another way, stationing troops on foreign soil demonstrates commitment in a way that rapid power projection capabilities cannot.

The relatively weak deterrent power associated with late-arriving forces is probably less true in regions where the United States is bound by strong defense commitments. It is more credible that the United States will deploy large forces over a period of months to Europe, Korea, and Southwest Asia than to any other part of the world. Therefore, in these cases, the eventual arrival of later-arriving forces probably plays an important deterrent role.

Two cases illustrate powerfully the deterring effects of the local military balance. The first is the conflict between Libya and France over Chad between the years 1980 and 1983; the second is the Jordanian crisis of 1970.

HISTORICAL CASES

Chad, 1980 and 1983

This example is about as close as one can get to a natural experiment on the impact of the local military balance, because the players and the stakes were the same in 1980 as they were in 1983; only the defender's (France's) contribution to the local military balance changed. In addition, French global military capability remained the same between 1980 and 1983. The particulars are as follows:[7]

France and Libya had been at odds over the fate of Chad since it gained independence from France in 1960. Since independence, internal political rivals backed by different external powers vied for

---

[7]See Lorell (1989); Lemarchand (1981), pp. 414–438; Haley (1984); Huth (1988), pp. 97–104.

power during a long civil war. Libya had long-standing interests in Chad because of its mineral resources in the north, as well as longer-term ambitions of annexation. Consequently, Libya supported a rebel faction led by Goukouni in Chad's civil war. France provided economic and military aid to try to stabilize the government after independence. In August 1979, France finally agreed to withdraw its troops from Chad on the condition that a peacekeeping force led by the Organization of African Unity (OAU) take its place. Shortly after the French withdrawal, Libyan-backed rebels attacked the capital. Despite repeated warnings from France, along with the alerting of French forces stationed in France, Libya supported a large-scale invasion of northern Chad using 4,000 to 5,000 Libyan troops to back Goukouni. By December 1980, the capital city, N'djamena, was overrun, and the French-backed leader, Habre, was deposed. Hence, the initial French attempt at extended deterrence failed.

In January 1981, Qaddafi announced plans to merge Libya and Chad. This merger was opposed by neighboring African states. Consistent pressure from these states eventually forced Libya to withdraw its forces from Chad in November 1981. Shortly thereafter, Goukouni's Transitional National Union Government fell into disarray, and civil war quickly resumed, despite the presence of OAU peacekeeping forces. In June 1992, Habre succeeded in toppling the Goukouni government, thereby reversing the defeat of December 1980.

In the spring of 1983, Goukouni's forces, resupplied by Libyan arms, confronted Habre in a series of battles lasting throughout the summer. By early August, Libya substantially increased its support for Goukouni in an attempt to achieve a decisive victory. In August 1993, Libya sent 2,000 to 3,000 troops south into Chad, including armored forces, airlift support, and tactical air support. By mid-August, it appeared that Goukouni's forces were gaining the upper hand and would soon be in a position to threaten the capital in a repeat of the events of December 1980.

However, this time the French government took prompt action to deter the advance on Chad's capital. Within two days, between August 10 and August 13, over 1,000 French troops were airlifted to the capital. Throughout August, further French reinforcements arrived and were deployed into forward positions along a defensive line protecting the capital. Approximately 3,000 French troops, including ten advanced combat aircraft, were eventually deployed to Chad. To underscore these actions, French President Mitterand warned that, if French troops were engaged, they would not limit themselves to purely defensive retaliation. As a result, Libya halted further escalation of the conflict and did not confront French forces.

By August 1983, a military stalemate had been reached, resulting in diplomatic negotiations to end the long civil war. These negotiations dragged on for over three years without resolution. France initially withdrew its forces in 1984, only to reinsert them in 1986 when the negotiations threatened to break down. Early in 1987, the stalemate ended when Habre's forces decisively defeated Goukouni's forces, compelling Libya to withdraw from Chad altogether.

This confrontation illustrates many of the points concerning capability and deterrence discussed above. France's national military power was far greater than Libya's, but this did not dissuade Qaddafi from supporting rebel forces in their assault on Chad. The fact that France was a nuclear power also seemed to be of little significance. Moreover, in December 1980, rebel forces conquered the capital, despite repeated warnings from the French. The assault on the capital in August 1983 was a repeat of the events of December 1980; however, this time the French backed up their warnings with the rapid deployment of forces to Chad. The French deployment not only created a "tripwire," thus raising the possibility of more massive French involvement, it also materially shifted the local military balance against Goukouni's Libyan-backed forces, making a quick rebel assault on the capital difficult—unlike in December 1980.

Jordan, 1970

Another interesting example is Israel's successful attempt to deter significant Syrian intervention on behalf of the Palestine Liberation Organization (PLO) in the 1970 Jordanian civil war (see Blechman and Kaplan, 1978, pp. 257–288; Quandt, 1977; and Safron, 1991, pp. 450–456). In the wake of the June 1967 "Six-Day War," Palestinian guerrillas operating out of several neighboring Arab states, including Jordan, took up a popular armed struggle against Israeli control of the "occupied" territories. Tensions between the PLO and the Jordanian government reached a peak in September 1970 ("Black

September") when King Hussein established a provisional military government in Jordan to bring the PLO under tighter control. Although he opposed Israel's control of the occupied territories, King Hussein feared Israeli retaliation for PLO attacks against Israel emanating from Jordan. Intense fighting broke out between PLO and Jordanian forces in northern Jordan.

On September 20, Syrian President Atasi sent armored forces into Jordan to fight on behalf of the PLO over the objections of his Defense Minister, Hafiz al-Assad. In an effort to prevent the downfall of King Hussein, a moderate Arab from the Israeli perspective, Israel mobilized its forces in the Golan Heights and northern Israel and threatened to intervene if King Hussein's regime was threatened. Syrian forces withdrew several days later, most likely because of the mounting Israeli threat on their flank—although other factors played a part as well (e.g., the prospect of U.S. and Soviet intervention, the lack of Egyptian support for Syria, and the civil-military split within the ruling Ba'ath Party in Syria). With the Syrian withdrawal, PLO resistance quickly collapsed.

What makes this case particularly noteworthy is that the existence of superior Israeli military forces alone did not dissuade President Atasi from intervening prior to September 20. However, once Israeli forces moved into positions on the Syrian flank and were poised to attack, Defense Minister Assad ordered the withdrawal of Syrian forces (presumably overruling Atasi). Thus, Israel's latent military capability was discounted until its presence was felt by the mobilization and alerting of Israeli armored forces, giving Israel a credible capability to cut off rapidly Syrian forces operating in northern Jordan. This prompt denial capability apparently was decisive in Assad's decision to withdraw Syrian armored forces.

U.S. PUNISHMENT STRATEGY

Because even a prompt denial capability may not be sufficient to deter a highly motivated adversary, an additional threat to damage or punish him may be necessary. For punishment threats to be effective, the United States must threaten what the adversary values most.[8] This question has particular relevance now, because the United States will rely more on its conventional forces to deter regional adversaries. Therefore, fewer targets can be reliably and promptly destroyed, which means that care must be exercised to select them wisely.

The evidence of prior crises and the scholarly literature on regimes suggest strongly that most regional adversaries, especially nondemocratic ones, value the preservation of their political power more highly than the welfare of their populations. This means that punishment threats aimed at the welfare of the population and the civilian economy are not likely to be very effective for deterrence. Threats aimed at the political stability of the adversary's regime are more likely to be effective.

Nondemocratic regimes depend for their preservation on the support of specific organizations and individuals. In totalitarian regimes, these tend to be the internal security forces and special units of the military. In authoritarian regimes, security forces are also important, but so are other organizations that have some degree of autonomous political power. Classically, these institutions include industrialists and other prominent individuals in the private economy, religious authorities, and the military leadership. Threatening to destroy these regime supporters should have a substantial effect on the behavior of nondemocratic regimes.

In a punishment strategy intended to threaten regime stability, the individual leaders and inner circle can be threatened directly. The United States has been building a record of proceeding against these so-called "leadership" targets with mixed results. Manuel Noriega was an explicit target of Operation Urgent Fury; Qaddafi was an implicit target of the air strike on Libya; and Saddam Hussein was probably an implicit target during Operation Desert Storm. In one case, the United States succeeded; in one it missed narrowly; and in one (seemingly) the effort failed entirely.

---

[8]By the late 1960s, nuclear deterrence strategy did not need to come firmly to grips with this question, because nuclear weapons existed in sufficient number to permit targeting virtually everything of conceivable value. Even so, at the heart of nuclear strategy was the punishment threat to annihilate the Soviet Union's population and economy. As discussed before, this countervalue core represented a set of assumptions about the character of the Soviet regime.

The effects of these attempts have been unclear. Obviously, the vulnerability of Noriega did not stimulate him to diminish the intensity of his confrontation with the United States—a striking reflection of the power of internal politics to shape the strategic actions of states. The near miss of Qaddafi may or may not have caused him to reduce his support of terrorism. Unquestionably, he became less public about it. The threats to Hussein are similarly unclear. They may have deterred him from using chemical weapons, although he seemed to be ·a U.S. target regardless of whether he used those weapons.

However, one must insert a strong cautionary note. Although there are logical reasons to expect that these threats to leaders are potent, there are serious problems with targeting the opponent's leadership. First are the substantial legal and moral compunctions.[9] Second is the strategic consideration that U.S. Presidents may be more vulnerable than Third World leaders. If the United States makes a practice of leadership targeting, we must be prepared for it to be practiced on us.[10] Few national interests may be large enough to warrant such an exchange. Third, in many cases, we may not wish to implement a threat to an adversary's leadership because of the "devil you know" phenomenon. The loss of a leader can produce consequences that may be even less desirable than the actions the United States seeks to deter. Finally, leadership targeting can be very difficult operationally, as the U.S. attempts have shown.

For these reasons, a related target set may be more attractive than leadership targets. We call them "regime-stability" targets. These are the organizations and individuals responsible for preserving the power of the regime, e.g., internal security forces, special military units, wealthy oligarchs, etc. Usually these have some sort of infrastructure that can be attacked, e.g., in the case of security forces,

---

[9]Assassination of foreign leaders is illegal in the United States. The limits of the definition of "assassination" are unclear. For example, does the law apply in the case of a declared war? What is its application in cases of undeclared wars? What constitutes a declared war in the post–Cold War period? Does "assassination" refer only to actions taken with certain weapons and tactics and not with others? For example, is it germane that in one case a sniper rifle be used and in another a tactical aircraft?

[10]The alleged Iraqi plot to kill former President Bush while on a trip to Kuwait may be an indication of this.

there may be barracks, vehicle parks, weapon and ammunition depots, etc. Also, these targets are usually disseminated widely, so they or the connections between them are difficult to protect.

The arguments we have mustered for punishment by regime targeting are based largely on logic. Nevertheless, there are historical cases that illustrate how sensitive states are to threats of this type. As the following discussion illustrates, threats to regimes can trigger frenzied activity in the adversary. That frenzy may be evidence of pain with deterrent value. However, that pain can also lead to desperate behavior that may be undesirable to the deterring state as the adversary reacts sharply to neutralize the threat. The reaction of the Syrian leadership to U.S. threats to topple its regime in 1957 provides an interesting historical example of the kinds of behavior one might elicit with the aforementioned punishment strategy.

In March of 1957, the United States entered into what was known as the Eisenhower doctrine. This policy provided for U.S. support of all kinds, including force, to friendly regimes in the Middle East endangered by the Soviets or their proxies. Though not explicitly identified as a particular target of the policy, Nasser's leadership and promotion of the Arab nationalist movement was the main stimulus for its promulgation. The U.S. hope was that the Eisenhower Doctrine would not only be a source of direct defense of allies but also a source of effective deterrence of Soviet and Arab nationalist activities in the region, particularly in Iraq, Lebanon, Libya, Jordan, Saudi Arabia, and Syria.

Jordan had just survived a crisis in 1956 and early 1957 in which King Hussein had successfully suppressed what were deemed to be anti-Western, pro-Communist, Arab-nationalist elements in his population and in the inner circles of his regime. He was able to carry this off with the help of Iraq and Saudi Arabia, backed by the United States.

In the summer of 1957, the United States endeavored to achieve a similar success in Syria. Syria, under Kassem, had been strongly supportive of Nasser and, in 1956, had begun to develop defense ties with the Soviet Union. The Syrian government, an authoritarian regime, was composed of a number of different factions, some friendly to Nasser and the Soviets, some much less so. What alarmed the United States was the prospect that the pro-Nasserite elements and Communists might seize complete control and carry Syria off to the Soviet camp.

To prevent that from happening, the United States issued a series of threats to the Syrian leadership warning of the consequences of increased ties to the Soviets and Egyptians. Indeed, the language of these threats explicitly stated that the United States would take action against the Syrian regime as punishment for the proscribed behavior. Apparently, more than mere threats were involved, because, in August 1957, the Syrians foiled a serious coup of opposition military officers who were supported by Turkey, Iraq, and Jordan, again likely backed by the United States.

The Syrians reacted to the conspiracy by declaring several members of the U.S. diplomatic community *persona non grata*. They also pressed the Soviets for increased shipments of weapons. The United States responded by arms deliveries of its own to Jordan and Lebanon and by a concentration of the Sixth Fleet off the Syrian coast. Most important, President Eisenhower called upon the Syrian people directly "to act to allay the anxiety caused by recent events"— in other words, to revolt and depose the Syrian regime.

The Syrian government reacted with frantic requests for help from Egypt and the Soviet Union, as well as other Arab states. Unfortunately, the character and explicitness of the threat to the Syrian regime were too blatant for Iraq and Saudi Arabia to ignore publicly, and these states (which had supported U.S. policy in Jordan) now sided with Syria. Seeing that the United States had miscalculated and was overextended, the Soviet Union took the opportunity to declare its readiness to defend the cause of Arab solidarity, thereby "proving" its willingness to balance U.S. power in the region. The Egyptians, similarly emboldened, sent two battalions to Syria, which became the nucleus for a combined Egyptian-Syrian armed force. Although the crisis subsided in November 1957, the Syrian "trauma" precipitated the rapid formation of the United Arab Republic in February 1958 a strengthening of ties between Egypt and Syria.

One might say with justification that the clumsy U.S. threats to the Syrian regime produced the worst possible results. But, for our purposes, the point to be noted is the potency of regime-stability threats.

Secure regimes are not so sensitive. Regimes like Syria's and most other regional adversaries are not secure and, hence, are highly sensitive to this form of pressure. The question is whether such threats can be used more constructively in the current era. Certainly, the absence of the Soviet Union removes one avenue of protection for threatened regional regimes. Nevertheless, regime-stability threats must almost always be kept private or implicit.

MILITARY CAPABILITIES

Conventional Forces

Even a favorable local or immediate military balance does not guarantee successful extended deterrence. Regional adversaries may not correctly perceive the balance (e.g., the effectiveness of modern air power in the recent Gulf War), or they may simply be overconfident about their ability to defeat local U.S. and allied forces. Such misperceptions may not be a product of ignorance (although this is always possible) but rather are inherent in the use of conventional military forces as instruments for deterrence. The deployment of conventional forces to a region is costly, ponderous, and complex, making it less likely that such actions will be taken. The outcomes of conventional wars, unlike those of nuclear wars, depend on numerous factors that are difficult to measure. These factors include military doctrine, tactics, accurate intelligence information, the skill and training of the troops, unit cohesion, generalship, terrain and weather, and technology. Luck often plays no small part in the success of conventional campaigns. Even when abundant information exists, as was the case between NATO and the Warsaw Pact during the Cold War, assessing the conventional military balance has proven to be very difficult. Witness the debates within the United States over whether or not NATO could successfully defend against a conventional attack by the Warsaw Pact.[11] Moreover, conventional military capabilities are constantly changing through advances in armor, avionics, sensors, munitions, etc.

---

[11]For example, see the discussions in Mearsheimer (1983), pp. 165–188, and Mako (1983).

Under these circumstances, it is not hard to understand why senior political and military leaders have a difficult time accurately assessing the likely outcome of conventional military operations. The destructiveness of nuclear weapons is clear. The delivery of such weapons is more akin to an engineering problem than to the complex logistics and operational issues associated with conventional military operations. This suggests that, if the United States is constrained to use only conventional military forces to deter regional adversaries, deterrence will be less reliable than it would be if credible nuclear threats could be made. Unfortunately, nuclear threats are probably not credible except under the specific circumstances discussed below.

Can anything be done to ameliorate this problem of the effectiveness of conventional deterrence? Here we move beyond the data that case studies can supply to the realm of logic and plausibility. The United States would benefit from making conventional forces as "transparent" in their capabilities as possible. Of course, one way to do this would be to fight periodic wars.[12] However, it would be preferable by far for the United States to communicate its conventional military capabilities more clearly through an intense, continuous program of realistic exercises and demonstrations more potent than annual TEAM SPIRITs and BRIGHT STARs. This program would be especially effective if it could be tailored to counter what an adversary hopes is a U.S. vulnerability. For example, an adversary hoping to move more quickly than the United States might be impressed with a demonstration of U.S. prompt denial capability. Similarly, an adversary hoping to enmesh U.S. forces in prepared defenses might be discouraged by a realistic demonstration of U.S. capabilities to deal with prepared defenses quickly and cheaply.

In addition, the United States could advertise some weapon system operational test and evaluation results. The point is not to subvert these activities by turning them into public-relations campaigns, but simply to note that some of these tests should be constructed so as to influence potential future adversaries. Public demonstrations of precision-guided weapons landing within several feet of their aim-

---

[12]This is the conclusion reached by Lieberman (1994). According to Lieberman, short-term deterrence failures may be a necessary part of the learning process that leads to long-term deterrence stability.

point or of the Joint Surveillance and Target Attack Radar System locating armored forces or convoys might send a strong message to regional adversaries that the United States can and will locate enemy forces and destroy them rapidly. The United States might also undertake joint exercises with regional allies and friends on a more frequent basis, especially if an adversary looms on the horizon.

There are difficulties with this approach. First, it may be difficult to design exercises so they do not appear provocative, hence setting off a spiral of regional tensions and/or arms buildups.[13] Second, a high level of tests and training exercises would be expensive. Israel is a good example of a state that conducts frequent training exercises and maintains a very high operational readiness to enhance Israel's reputation for prompt military action. This boosts the credibility of Israel's conventional deterrent, but it costs them dearly in terms of government spending.[14] Although the United States may not need to match the Israeli operational tempo, exercises and tests should be viewed as one way to convey a deterrent message apart from their objective of honing warfighting skills and evaluating the engineering performance of weapon systems.

Nuclear Weapons

Even with a demonstration program along the lines suggested above, conventional forces will probably never be as deterring as nuclear weapons. Nuclear forces simply are inherently more impressive and clear in their destructiveness. For this reason, we believe it is important for the United States not to permit an adversary to be absolutely sure the United States would *never* use nuclear weapons in a regional conflict under any circumstance.

The problem is to make this threat credible. Just as regional adversaries tend to discount the mobilization potential of a great power, they also tend to discount its nuclear capability if they suspect that

---

[13]Jervis (1976), pp. 58–113, discusses the provocation problem.

[14]The Israeli situation is slightly different, because it involves central deterrence. In addition, Israel relies to some extent on its undeclared nuclear capability to deter threats to Israel's homeland. For a discussion of Israeli conventional deterrence policy, see Shimshoni (1988).

political and moral constraints will preclude nuclear use.[15]   In the U.S. case, this belief is encouraged by a pledge under the Nuclear Non-Proliferation Treaty not to threaten nonnuclear states with nuclear attack, along with unilateral U.S. declarations buttressing this pledge in the United Nations.

There are three limited situations in which U.S. nuclear threats against regional adversaries may remain credible:

• In response to an adversary's first use of nuclear weapons

• In response to an adversary's use of chemical or biological weapons[16]

• In response to an adversary's threat to overwhelm a major U.S. ground unit, even if that threat is entirely conventional.

The first two situations, when an adversary threatens to employ nuclear weapons or some other weapon of mass destruction, are discussed in a companion document to this report and, hence, will not be discussed further here (see Wilkening and Watman, 1994). The third situation is when important U.S. interests are threatened by an adversary that may not be defeatable at an acceptable cost by purely conventional means. Historical examples in which implicit nuclear threats were made include the 1961 Berlin crisis and the 1954 Quemoy-Matsu crisis between the United States and China.[17]

---

[15]The essential irrelevance of nuclear weapons can be seen in the Falklands War and the conflict between France and Libya over Chad. In both cases, regional aggression occurred despite the fact that the defender was a nuclear power. When we recall these crises, it seems highly implausible to think that either Great Britain or France would have made nuclear threats in an attempt to compel Argentina or Libya to accept the status quo *ante*, much less actually carry out these threats if they refused.

[16]The gray area represented by chemical or biological weapons is particularly troublesome for U.S. strategy, because the United States will soon eliminate its chemical weapons. U.S. biological weapons were eliminated years ago. Hence, the United States cannot rely on tit-for-tat retaliatory threats to deter chemical or biological attacks. U.S. leaders could threaten conventional escalation, perhaps by expanding the war aims to include the capture and later trial of the leaders responsible for these attacks as war criminals. Threatening to use nuclear weapons is the other alternative. Obviously, the utility of U.S. nuclear threats in such circumstances is in tension with a "no first use" policy.

[17]In the Quemoy-Matsu crisis the United States had substantial naval forces deployed in the straits between Taiwan and the mainland, in addition to its nuclear capability. Hence, the local military balance may have favored the United States, thereby

Obviously, the last nuclear employment situation—forestalling the defeat of a major U.S. combat unit—is most open to skepticism. Would it be credible to threaten what would be nuclear first use against an adversary that had not used any weapon of mass destruction—and perhaps did not even possess any? There is no way of answering this question, but it seems plausible that, especially in the early period of an intervention, U.S. light ground units may find themselves in dire straits. If the United States has no other means to save them from being overrun and the tactical conditions are appropriate, a U.S. President might convincingly threaten to do "all that is necessary" to protect them, rather than passively accept the human and political costs of their destruction. This said, the central point is that, in the vast majority of purely conventional conflicts, the United States may not encounter the conditions needed to make U.S. nuclear threats credible against regional adversaries.

For political reasons, not the least of which is to avoid provoking other countries to acquire nuclear weapons to deter the United States, the United States should be exceedingly circumspect about mentioning the use of nuclear weapons against a nonnuclear adversary. U.S. declaratory policy should strongly emphasize the use of conventional military options (in addition to condemning the first use of nuclear, biological, or chemical weapons). The point here is simply that the United States should not create a situation in which an adversary believes, with a high degree of certainty, that the United States will *never* use nuclear weapons under any circumstance.

Implications for Regional Deterrence

Much has been covered in this chapter, and a short summary may be helpful. First, the most important military capability required for deterrence is to be able to deny the adversary his or her objective. Prompt denial, the capability to prevent the adversary from reaching an objective, is more deterring than a rollback capability to be employed after the adversary has captured his or her objective. The relevant military forces for a prompt denial capability are those sta-

---

contributing to successful deterrence. Another opinion holds that China never intended to attack and, hence, that this is not an example of extended deterrence success but rather a nondeterrence event.

tioned in the theater or those that can arrive in time to interpose themselves between the adversary and his objective. If U.S. national military strategy is designed with regional deterrence in mind, "forward presence" and/or rapid "crisis response" become key elements in this strategy.[18]

Second, the United States could profitably develop a program of exercises and demonstrations to make its conventional capabilities as transparent as possible.

Third, the United States should retain some thread of nuclear threat in its regional deterrence strategy to be used on those specific occasions when such a threat is likely to be credible.

---

[18]Again, "rapid" means that the United States must be able to credibly deny an opponent's war aims on a timetable set by the adversary. If an adversary believes he can conquer a neighboring state within a week, the time frame for a U.S. response is days. If it takes several days for an adversary to accomplish his military objectives, then 24 to 48 hours is the time frame for a rapid U.S. response.

Chapter Six

GENERAL OBSERVATIONS REGARDING REGIONAL DETERRENCE

The research findings discussed bear on the "requirements" for regional deterrence: If the United States wishes to deter a regional adversary with high confidence, what are the requirements to be met? However, this begs a critical question that arises with the end of the Cold War: To what extent *should* the United States rely on deterrence to protect its regional interests? This question could never have been asked during the Cold War. At that time, deterring the Soviet Union was the focus of U.S. national security strategy. Deterrence was not an option—it was a necessity, since nuclear war was inconceivable.

In the post–Cold War era, this may not be true with respect to deterring some types of regional adversaries. There are likely to be some regional adversaries against whom and some occasions when the United States may elect *not* to implement deterrence. The more costly and difficult deterrence is found to be, the more often the United States may choose not to use deterrence in its regional security strategies. Instead, alternative policies, such as appeasement or neglect, may be more desirable. Indeed, it may be more cost-effective for the United States to fight an occasional war with a particular regional adversary than to pursue a costly, concerted, and unremitting policy of deterrence. For, in the final analysis, deterrence is an *option* now, not a necessity. As such, it needs to be evaluated using the same metrics of cost and benefit that are applied to all other strategic options. Deterrence is no longer sacrosanct.

INTELLIGENCE

Our findings suggest that regional adversaries are more or less difficult to deter depending upon their motivations for entering into the crisis with the United States. If an adversary is motivated more by a desire for gain than to avert loss and if his status quo is more satisfactory than not, such an adversary will fall into the easier-to-deter category. If an adversary is motivated by a desire to avert loss and if his status quo and prospects are less satisfactory, such an adversary will fall into the harder-to-deter category. We use this categorization for convenience, since we understand that, in reality, regional adversaries are arrayed along a deterrence continuum.

One of the fundamental contributions of national intelligence is to help decisionmakers understand in which category (or place on the continuum) a particular regional adversary falls. Its particular location on that continuum will shape importantly the requirements the United States needs to meet to deter successfully. In particular, there is a critical need for accurate political intelligence regarding the stability of political regimes governing Third World states, since the desire to avert the loss of domestic political power frequently leads to risk-taking behavior. This, in turn, implies that these states may be hard to deter. For the most part, this type of intelligence is collected by signal and human intelligence sources and methods. Imagery is probably less important. It is unclear to us how well prepared the U.S. intelligence community is to acquire and analyze such data.

This point has particular salience at a time of defense reductions. The smaller U.S. military capability is, the more efficient must be the allocation of that capability to its tasks. Inefficiency threatens to increase dangerously the chances that some demands on U.S. forces will not be met. Among the efficiencies is what is called "economy of force": assigning to each task only as much force as needed and no more. In the context of deterrence, this means gauging correctly how difficult an adversary will be to deter. Failure to do so will mean underdeterring the difficult and overdeterring the easy.

STRATEGIES AND CAPABILITIES

For adversaries in the easier-to-deter category, the research suggests that deterrence requirements are often moderate. Such adversaries can be deterred by posing a reasonably credible threat of U.S. involvement in the event of a crisis. Strategies that communicate or signal this threat are an appropriate choice in these cases. A "tripwire" strategy is a good example. The tripwire force cannot itself defend the U.S. interest threatened by the regional adversary. But a symbolic force is sufficient to deny the adversary a reasonable hope of a "free ride." Given the low risk-taking propensities of these adversaries, denial of a "free ride" can be a very effective deterrent. Indeed, such adversaries may be quite responsive to deterrence strategies that fall short even of a tripwire.

The capabilities needed for a symbolic deterrence strategy emphasize "presence" in some form. The symbol of U.S. intention to defend an interest is usually a military force insufficient to defend the interest. That force must be tied with the interest to be defended, either through basing in the area or through visits. The visits must be sufficiently frequent that the adversary cannot reliably hope to conclude his operation without a significant risk of encountering the U.S. symbolic force. An example of such a strategy is "presence," such as that provided by the U.S. Navy. An offshore presence cannot deny a motivated enemy its objective; however, the presence of naval forces does pose a threat of U.S. involvement, which may be sufficiently credible to make the threatened U.S. interest an unattractive target of opportunity for potential regional adversaries. The logic of this argument suggests that naval presence is likely to be less effective than a ground presence, because an adversary can better entertain the possibility that it will not have to engage the former. Air forces probably fall between these two, if they are introduced into the crisis area. That done, air forces would be less avoidable than naval forces, though still more "withdrawable" than ground forces.

In sum, the requirements for deterring these sorts of regional adversaries are moderate, even considering the resource constraints expected to shape U.S. military capabilities for the foreseeable future.

The same cannot be said for the harder-to-deter regional adversaries. Motivated often by major domestic concerns, these adversaries require more than a symbolic strategy for successful deterrence. Our research suggests that what is required is a highly credible capability to deny them their political and military objectives promptly and, in some cases, to punish them by threatening regime-stability targets.

The capabilities needed to implement a prompt denial strategy of deterrence, with or without an additional capability to punish, are likely to be large and expensive. Most stressing may be a requirement for forward forces sufficient to stop the adversary short of his objective, at least until additional forces can arrive. Optimally, this means stationing all the forces necessary between the adversary and his objective, but even the United States lacks the resources to meet such a requirement in more than a few cases simultaneously. Therefore, a strong incentive exists for the United States to explore capabilities that can provide prompt denial and that are so rapidly deployable into an area as to be "virtually" stationed there. Air forces are a natural choice for this sort of capability, at least against threats vulnerable to air attack.

The military capabilities needed to punish an adversary by endangering his regime stability are varied. Presumably, the capability to strike reliably with precision and surprise from long distances will be important. This is because attacking the regime-supporting organizations and installations likely will require low collateral damage, multiple attacks (since the targets may be widely disseminated), and low cost (to enhance the credibility of the threat).

Special operation forces may also be useful, for two reasons. First, they may be the only way to strike at targets that are commingled with civilian areas. Second, such forces (specifically, Army Special Forces) may be very useful for training internal insurgencies in the state we wish to deter. Regional adversaries frequently contain dissident populations. On some occasions, it may be very useful for purposes of deterrence to threaten to increase the power of those dissident populations.

POLITICAL CONSTRAINTS

There are significant constraints in the way of satisfying these military requirements. Some of these constraints are political.

The U.S. government is not designed for swift action, even when the president can act unilaterally. Normally, presidential inhibitions on the commitments of the United States make it difficult to meet the "promptness" requirement. This difficulty is exacerbated greatly by the internal and external coalitions that the United States often must form as a prerequisite to international military action. Internal coalitions refer to the congressional and popular support necessary to permit the deployment of U.S. troops (at least in large numbers). External coalitions refer to the increasingly multinational character of international military action. While, in principle, the United States can act unilaterally, it is likely to opt to do so less and less often.

Traditionally, the United States has coped with this sort of problem by using commitment and the activities easily identified as committing. For example, the United States does as much as possible to persuade the adversary that all the preparation and coalition-building needed for a prompt response have been accomplished prior to any crisis. Contingency plans have been created, forces earmarked, training adapted, exercises formulated, and "red lines" agreed to by all concerned. Therefore, when a crisis does arise, only presidential authorization is necessary to commit the forces. The adversary is given no reason to hope that much, if any, crisis coalition-building will slow the U.S. response. This is the logic of our commitment to South Korea, Europe, and, to some extent, the Persian Gulf. Unfortunately, this process of preparation is feasible in only a limited number of areas. Further, since commitment of this sort drastically reduces freedom of action, the United States likely will reserve it for only the most important interests. Therefore, for most places, most of the time, prompt action by the United States is unlikely.

A second type of political constraint is that imposed by fears of the public's reputed sensitivity to U.S. casualties. We say "reputed" because, as discussed earlier, other research carried out under this project suggests that the reality of U.S. sensitivity to casualties may be quite different from the prevailing wisdom.[1]

These findings may not apply to public sensitivity to *anticipated* casualties as a crisis deepens, since the data used are almost entirely extracted from public opinion polling once fighting has begun and U.S. casualties have accrued. In this regard, one could argue reasonably that the public's precombat sensitivity to casualties may be dif-

---

[1]See Schwarz (1994).

ferent from its sensitivity once combat has begun. To this we can only say, "possibly so." But it is clear that the issue of casualty sensitivity is much more complex than today's common wisdom that Americans simply will not tolerate casualties. Prior experience suggests otherwise and that casualty sensitivity may be related to the magnitude of the U.S. interest at stake.

It is important that the U.S. conversation with itself about this question be much clearer and more accurate. Saying unconditionally, as many do, that the U.S. public will not tolerate casualties is to provide potential adversaries with dangerously incorrect information. For example, this may have affected Saddam Hussein's risk calculations. Therefore, it behooves the defense community to treat this matter with greater care, if for no other reason than to avoid undermining our own deterrence efforts.

A last type of political constraint specifically affects the proposed punishment strategy. Threatening to attack the stability of regional regimes can produce substantial discomfort in coalition partners, as well as within the United States, regardless of how effective such threats may be for deterrence. This is especially true if the adversary's leadership itself is among the targets.

This problem may be of particular importance to the extent the United States seeks to rely on the threat of punishment to substitute for, rather than complement, the threat of prompt denial. This would be a very tempting way to circumvent the sizable and expensive requirements imposed by prompt denial. It would be much easier if the United States could deter reliably by threatening to strike important targets of the adversary, even though its military capabilities are left substantially intact.

As mentioned, experience is not encouraging to the hope that punishment alone can deter. However, that experience was gained at earlier times with much less effective weapons against very highly motivated adversaries. It may be that the threat of modern capabilities wielded for punishment against less-motivated adversaries may be more effective. At this point, there is no more that can be said on an empirical basis. We think this question of denial versus punishment is a promising and important one for additional research.

MILITARY CONSTRAINTS

At least as weighty are the military constraints impeding the U.S. ability and desire to meet the requirements for deterring the harder-to-deter cases. Under the pressure of resource reductions, many U.S. military trends are running counter to the policies recommended here for regional deterrence.

First, the United States is reducing its overseas deployments, particularly in Europe. Europe may no longer urgently require U.S. deterrence protection, although that is far from clear yet. The general trend toward continental U.S. basing undermines deterrence extended to other regions, because it undermines prompt denial.

Second, the United States does not now use exercises and demonstrations as a means of deterrence communication, at least to the extent we suggest. Indeed, the size and frequency of some U.S. exercises are in danger of reduction, for example, TEAM SPIRIT. In addition, operational tempo rates are declining for all three services when a higher level of activity focused on specific regions would be desirable for deterrence.

Third, the notion of punishment may be at odds with the trend toward increasingly precise and "bloodless" war. Operations intended to threaten regime stability may not imply great collateral damage, but they are not likely to be antiseptic.

Fourth, to support nonproliferation, the United States is moving in the direction of deemphasizing the role of nuclear weapons. This may be a reasonable policy when all U.S. policy objectives are considered. However, with respect solely to regional deterrence, an entirely nonnuclear regional strategy is likely to be counterproductive.

These trends are driven by good reasons: the end of the Cold War and a declining defense budget. We are not proposing here that the trends be reversed. However, we are pointing out that a substantial deterrence price is likely paid.

DETERRENCE IN U.S. REGIONAL STRATEGY

Deterrence of the easier-to-deter adversaries is within U.S. capabilities for the foreseeable future. However, the harder-to-deter adversaries are a different matter. Given the difficulty of deterring these adversaries, the focused and long-term application of effort and resources necessary, and the limits on those resources, the United States will be able to devote its deterrence attention to only a small number of these adversaries. Presumably, this number will be smaller than the number the United States would prefer to deter. Unfortunately, some number of the harder-to-deter adversaries will have to be treated as though they were among the easier-to-deter adversaries, implying that the United States will use limited presence, perhaps tripwires, but not a credible prompt denial and punishment capability to deter hostile acts. So treated, some number of these adversaries will be deterred. Most, sooner or later, will not. Therefore, the United States has to focus its deterrence strategy very carefully so as to be able to concentrate its efforts on the most important interests and to make sure it can tolerate the consequences of the failure to deter other harder-to-deter adversaries.

THE ROLE OF HISTORICAL EVIDENCE

We have used historical data in several different ways to support this research.

First, we conducted an extensive review of the deterrence literature, which consists of two bodies of work, the classical, deductive development of deterrence theory and the later, empirical, inductive assessment of deterrence practice in international politics. The latter relies on history for data, and, as a result, most of the empirical research is accompanied by detailed case studies of crises in which deterrence was deemed to play a part. We studied these cases carefully and, in some instances, elaborated on them to develop our hypotheses about regional deterrence.

Second, one of our principal hypotheses concerns the links between the governing regimes of regional adversaries, their domestic political problems, and their propensity to accept risk. Few of the case studies we consulted contained detailed information addressing these factors. Therefore, we elaborated a number of those cases with additional information bearing on the specific areas of interest to us.

Third, the research literature on deterrence (academic and otherwise) provides a number of propositions about deterrence for which there is some support in evidence. However, these do not exist in the context of an overall model of deterrence; indeed, a number of the supported propositions are in conflict with one another. These include the following:

- Deterrence is an invalid concept, since adversaries often do not *choose* to enter a conflict. Others believe that deterrence is a valid concept, since adversaries do have sufficient choice to enter or refrain from a conflict.

- Military capabilities are only weakly related to deterrence outcomes, as opposed to the view that military capabilities are strongly related to deterrence outcome.

- Demonstrating commitment is the primary determinant of deterrence success, as opposed to the view that commitment is important but does not determine deterrence success.

To resolve these contending views, we delved into the existing cases in considerable depth. By that process, we found strong support for the views developed in the study:

- Most adversaries do not enter conflict entirely out of a sense of compulsion. They retain sufficient choice over their behavior that deterrence is a valid concept in dealing with them.

- Local military capabilities are of great importance in deterrence success.

- Commitment or resolve is important but no more so than local military capabilities.

Fourth, we used historical examples throughout to illustrate and "flesh out" the conceptual issues raised in the research.

THE JAPANESE DECISION TO ATTACK PEARL HARBOR

The Japanese decision to enter into war with the United States and Great Britain represents a classic example of the sort of decisionmaking driven by assessments of the costs of inaction. It is a profitable case to study not only because it is a striking example of risk assessment under extreme conditions, but also because it illustrates well some of the factors at play (in a less extreme way) in the decision-making of more commonly encountered regional adversaries.[1]

In the Japanese government of the time, decisions as to whether or not to go to war were the formal province of the cabinet. However, the bulk of the deliberations prior to cabinet considerations was conducted in the Liaison Conferences attended by a committee of high military and civilian government leaders. A somewhat expanded National Security Council is the best U.S. analogy to this Japanese organization. The Liaison Conference sessions were attended by the Prime Minister, Foreign Minister, Navy Minister, War Minister, the Chiefs of Staff of the Army and Navy, their Deputy Chiefs, and assorted high-level civilians representing economic ministries. This committee met several times during the latter half of 1941 and reached the decision to take Japan into war. The accounts of these meetings are available virtually in stenographic form, and they provide a remarkable look into the analytical processes employed by the participants (Ike, 1967). As always, these processes

---

[1]This discussion of the Japanese decisionmaking relies generally on several sources. See Wohlstetter (1962); Betts (1982); Morton (1954), pp. 1325–1337; Sagan (1988); Toland (1970); Maxon (1957); Hearings Before the Joint Committee on the Investigation of the Pearl Harbor Attack (1946); and Ike (1967).

were a mixture of clarity and chaos, detachment and manic passion. But, in our view, what comes through clearly was the sentiment that the almost certain costs of inaction for Japan exceeded the uncertain, although potentially very high, costs of action. For the most part, the participants understood Japan's weaknesses and the implications of U.S. strengths. The overall level of self-delusion and impetuousness, while undoubtedly present, seems low. Rather, even the most pessimistic Japanese officials seem to have believed that the current and prospective status quo for Japan was inconsistent with her most vital objectives—membership among the Great Powers with an established sphere of interest—and that the only course of action open to Japan with any chance of success (even if low) was war.

On July 2, 1941, the Japanese cabinet endorsed the view developed in the Liaison Conferences that Japan had to develop the Greater Asia Co-Prosperity Sphere to include all British, Dutch, French, and Portuguese possessions in the Far East, as well as the Philippines, India, and Australia. Although leaving open the prospect of achieving these objectives by negotiation, the minutes of the meeting are explicit that the Co-Prosperity Sphere was to be pursued "no matter what obstacles may be encountered" and "no matter what international developments take place."[2] Indeed, the decision memorandum refers explicitly to the necessity of an "advance into the Southern Regions." The Japanese decisionmakers hoped that the United States could be kept out of this war, but they accepted the necessity of planning for the disappointment of those hopes.

The Liaison Conference met again on October 23 to consider whether or not the United States could be kept out of a war while Japan pursued the Co-Prosperity Sphere. The conferees agreed that there was no chance that the United States would accept Japanese objectives in the Far East and drop its economic sanctions. They further agreed that compliance with U.S. terms to resolve the sanctions crisis would mean that "Japan would be compelled ultimately to withdraw entirely from the (Asian) continent." At the same time, the conference concluded that it was not possible for Japan to fight the United States separately, that U.S. war potential was seven or eight times that of Japan, and that "there were no means of directly van-

---

[2]Quoted in Wohlstetter (1962), p. 346.

quishing the United States in case of war against her."[3]   Yet, this conference reached a unanimous or, at least, majority decision to go to war with the United States if negotiations were unavailing—as all expected them to be. Why was this decision made?

The military members of the Liaison Conference were quite optimistic that Japan could achieve major successes in the Pacific against the United States and Britain in the first six to twelve months of war. However, they were equally pessimistic about Japanese chances if the war continued beyond that point. This assessment was entirely realistic.   On the other hand, they believed that continuation of diplomatic activities was foolish, since they were unlikely to bear fruit and would erode even Japan's short-term advantages as U.S. war preparedness accelerated. Therefore, as Navy Minister Shimada concluded, "though there is a great risk in beginning the war now, we must realize that there is also great risk in depending on negotiations unless we can be certain of the final outcome."[4]

Ultimately, the Japanese chose war in the hopes that, in some way, it could be kept short. But, as they were aware, they had no plan to ensure that it would be short, other than to hope that the United States would elect to cut its losses in an area of the world of less interest than Europe.   In other words, the Japanese could not deprive the United States of the freedom of action or the means to continue the conflict.   The Japanese chose this course—which U.S. planners discounted as grossly irrational—because all other courses seemed worse.[5]

Indeed, as Roberta Wohlstetter has pointed out, the very notion of "choice" is slippery in such situations (Wohlstetter, 1962, p. 357). The Japanese felt compelled to go to war; they did not see themselves as free *not* to do so. This notion of compulsion occurs frequently in the assessments of states in similar circumstances and illustrates the difficulty of even less extreme, more common international situations. Inherent in the concept of deterrence is that the adversary has some freedom to refrain from the undesirable behavior. If he thinks

---

[3]Togo (1956), pp. 125–127.

[4]Quoted in Wohlstetter (1962) p. 351.

[5]Quoted in Sagan (1988), pp. 894, 904.

he has none, deterrence must fail. If he thinks he has at least some freedom to refrain (as most states do), deterrence is possible even if difficult.

A final point is in order about the problem these situations pose to U.S. intelligence analysts. The assessments of U.S. planners about the consequences of war with Japan were identical to those of the Japanese. The U.S. estimate found the disparities in national power to be so great that "national sanity would dictate against such an event" (referring to war).[6] But this U.S. conclusion omitted an assessment of the status quo and its future prospects as viewed by the Japanese and provides a good illustration of how frequently such considerations are dropped from deterrence calculations. The United States never weighed seriously the Japanese view that the alternative to war was "gradual exhaustion" without ever having struck a single blow (Wohlstetter, 1962, p. 354).

Interestingly, as desperate as the Japanese believed their situation to be, they clearly were deterrable, at least in a limited military sense. Admiral Nagumo, the commander of the Japanese naval force sent to attack Pearl Harbor, was under orders to abort the operation if his approach was detected. The Japanese planners believed that surprise was essential if the attack was to have any prospect for success. Therefore, the United States could have deterred the Japanese by taking steps that suggested to them that surprise had been lost.

North Korea and Cuba are current candidates for nondeterrable status. Both are facing prospects that appear catastrophic for the survival of the existing political regimes. The forces pushing in this direction seem irresistible if left unremediated. Remediation, in these cases, would require some benign, external intervention to shore up these regimes in much the way the Soviets did. This seems unlikely, short of coercion by the failing regime. So far as we know, Cuba has no coercive means sufficient to this task. Humanitarian intervention can be expected in Cuba, but nowhere near the magnitude needed to preserve the Castro regime. North Korea, on the other hand, has managed to create better prospects by skillfully us-

---

[6]Hearings Before the Joint Committee on the Investigation of the Pearl Harbor Attack (1946), Part 14, p. 1056.

ing its putative nuclear capability to extort economic and diplomatic benefits from Japan, South Korea, and the United States. Whether it can extort enough to make a difference is an open question.

BIBLIOGRAPHY

Achen, Christopher, and Duncan Snidal, "Rational Deterrence Theory and Comparative Case Studies," *World Politics*, January 1989.

Adomeit, H., "Soviet Crisis Prevention and Management: Why and When Do Soviet Leaders Take Risks?" *Orbis*, Vol. 30, Spring 1986, pp. 55–56.

Almond, G., and J. Coleman, eds., *The Politics of Developing Areas*, Princeton: Princeton University Press, 1960.

Almond, G., and G. Powell, *Comparative Politics: A Developmental Approach*, Boston: Little, Brown, 1966.

Anderson, P., and T. McKeown, "Changing Aspirations, Limited Attention, and War," *World Politics*, Vol. 40, No. 1, 1987, pp. 17–22.

Apter, D., *The Politics of Modernization*, Chicago: University of Chicago Press, 1965.

Arquilla, John, *Dubious Battles: Aggression, Defeat, and the International System*, Washington, D.C.: Crane-Russak, 1992.

Ayoob, Mohammed, "The Security Problematic of the Third World," *World Politics*, Vol. 43, January 1991, pp. 257–283.

Betts, Richard, *Surprise Attack*, Washington, D.C.: Brookings Institution, 1982.

Blechman, B., and S. Kaplan, *Force Without War: U.S. Armed Forces as a Political Instrument*, Washington, D.C.: Brookings Institution, 1978.

Blondel, J., *Comparing Political Systems*, New York: Praeger, 1972.

Bull, Hedley, *The Anarchical Society: A Study of Order in World Politics*, New York: Columbia University Press, 1977.

Buzan, B., "People, States, and Fear: The National Security Problem in the Third World," in E. Azar and C. Moon, eds., *National Security in the Third World: The Management of Internal and External Threats*, Aldershot, England: Edward Elgar Publishing Limited, 1988, pp. 14–43.

Christensen, T., "Threats, Assurances, and the Last Chance for Peace: The Lessons of Mao's Korean War Telegrams," *International Security*, Summer 1992, pp. 122–154.

David, S., *Choosing Sides: Alignment and Realignment in the Third World*, Baltimore: Johns Hopkins University Press, 1991.

Davis, Paul K., "Improving Deterrence in the Post–Cold War Era: Some Theory and Implications for Defense Planning," in Paul K. Davis, ed., *New Challenges for Defense Planning: Rethinking How Much Is Enough*, Santa Monica, Calif.: RAND, MR-400-RC, 1994.

Davis, Paul K., and John Arquilla, *Deterring or Coercing Opponents in Crisis: Lessons from the War with Saddam Hussein*, Santa Monica, Calif.: RAND, R-4111-JS, 1991a.

Davis, Paul K., and John Arquilla, *Thinking About Opponent Behavior in Crisis and Conflict: A Generic Model for Analysis and Group Discussion*, Santa Monica, Calif.: RAND, N-3322-JS, 1991b.

Downs, George, "The Rational Deterrence Debate," *World Politics*, January 1989.

Doyle, Michael, "Liberalism and World Politics," *American Political Science Review*, December 1986.

Dror, Yehezkel, *Crazy States*, Millwood, N.Y.: Kraus Reprint, 1980.

Edwardes, M., *Nehru: A Political Biography*, New York: Praeger, 1972.

Elster, John, ed., *Rational Choice*, Oxford: Basil Blackwell Ltd, 1986.

"Falkland Islands—The Origins of a War," *The Economist*, June 19, 1982, p. 43.

Finer, S., *Comparative Government*, New York: Basic Books, 1971.

Fisher, M., L. Rose, and R. Huttenback, *Himalayan Battleground: Sino-Indian Rivalry in Ladakh*, London: Pall Mall, 1963.

Freedman, Lawrence, and Efraim Karsh, *The Gulf Conflict, 1990–1991: Diplomacy and War in the New World Order*, Princeton, N.J.: Princeton University Press, 1993.

Freedman, Lawrence, *The Evolution of Nuclear Strategy*, New York: St. Martin's Press, 1983.

George, A., ed., *Avoiding War: Problems of Crisis Management*, Boulder: Westview Press, 1991.

George, Alexander, and Richard Smoke, *Deterrence in American Foreign Policy: Theory and Practice*, New York: Columbia University Press, 1974.

Haley, P., *Qaddafi and the United States Since 1969*, New York: Praeger, 1984.

Halperin, M., *Limited War in the Nuclear Age*, New York: John Wiley & Sons, Inc., 1963.

Hastings, M., and S. Jenkins, *The Battle for the Falklands*, New York: W. W. Norton and Co., 1983.

Hearings Before the Joint Committee on the Investigation of the Pearl Harbor Attack, 79th Congress, Washington, D.C.: U.S. Government Printing Office, 1946.

Huth, Paul, *Extended Deterrence and the Prevention of War*, New Haven, Conn.: Yale University Press, 1988.

Huth, Paul, and Bruce Russett, "What Makes Deterrence Work? Cases from 1900–1980," *World Politics*, Vol. 36, 1984, pp. 496, 526.

Huth, Paul, and Bruce Russett, "Deterrence Failure and Crisis Escalation," *International Studies Quarterly*, Vol. 32, 1988, pp. 29–45.

Huth, Paul, and Bruce Russett, "Testing Deterrence Theory: Rigor Makes a Difference," *World Politics*, Vol. 42, 1990, pp. 466–501.

Huth, Paul, and Bruce Russett, "General Deterrence Between Enduring Rivals: Testing Three Competing Models," *American Political Science Review*, Vol. 87, March 1993.

Ike, N., ed., *Japan's Decision for War: Records of the 1941 Policy Conferences*, Stanford, Calif.: Stanford University Press, 1967.

Jackson, R., *Quasi-States: Sovereignty, International Relations, and the Third World*, New York: Cambridge University Press, 1993.

Jervis, Robert, *Perception and Misperception in International Politics*, Princeton: Princeton University Press, 1976.

Jervis, Robert, "Rational Deterrence: Theory and Evidence," *World Politics*, January 1989.

Jervis, Robert, Richard Lebow, and Janice Stein, *Psychology & Deterrence*, Baltimore: Johns Hopkins University Press, 1985.

Job, B., *The Insecurity Dilemma: National Security of the Third World State*, Boulder, Colorado: Lynne-Rienner Publishers, Inc., 1992.

Kahn, Herman, *On Escalation*, Baltimore: Penguin Books, 1965.

Kahneman, Daniel, Paul Slovak, and Amos Tversky, *Judgment Under Uncertainty: Heuristics and Biases*, Cambridge: Cambridge University Press, 1982.

Kahneman, Daniel, and Amos Tversky, "Prospect Theory: An Analysis of Decision Under Risk," *Econometrica*, Vol. 47, No. 2, March 1979, pp. 263–291.

Kaplan, S., *Diplomacy of Power*, Washington, D.C.: Brookings Institution, 1981.

Karsh, E., and I. Rautsi, "Why Saddam Hussein Invaded Kuwait," *Survival*, January/February 1991, pp. 18–30.

Kavic, L., *India's Quest for Security: Defense Policies, 1947–1965*, Berkeley: University of California Press, 1967.

Kennan, G., "The Sources of Soviet Conduct," in T. Etzold and J. Gaddis, eds., *Containment: Documents on American Policy and Strategy, 1945–1950*, New York: Columbia University Press, 1978.

Lamb, A., *The China-India Border: The Origins of the Disputed Boundaries*, London: Oxford University Press, 1964.

Lebow, Richard Ned, and Janice Stein, "Rational Deterrence Theory: I Think, Therefore I Deter," *World Politics*, January 1989.

Lebow, Richard Ned, "Miscalculation in the South Atlantic: The Origins of the Falklands War," in R. Jervis, R. Lebow, and J. Stein, *Psychology & Deterrence*, Baltimore: Johns Hopkins University Press, 1985, pp. 89–124.

Lebow, Richard Ned, *Between Peace and War: The Nature of International Crises*, Baltimore: Johns Hopkins University Press, 1981.

Lemarchand, R., "Chad: The Roots of Chaos," *Current History*, Vol. 80, 1981, pp. 414–438.

Levy, J., "Quantitative Studies of Deterrence Success and Failure," in R. Axelrod et al., eds., *Perspectives on Deterrence*, Washington, D.C.: National Academy of Science, National Research Council, 1988.

Lieberman, Elli, "The Rational Deterrence Theory Debate: Is the Dependent Variable Elusive?" *Security Studies*, London: Frank Cass, Spring 1994.

Linz, J., "Totalitarian and Authoritarian Regimes," in F. Greenstein and N. Polsby, eds., *Handbook of Political Science:* Vol. 3, *Macropolitical Theory*, Reading, Mass.: Addison-Wesley Publishing Co., 1975.

Lorell, M. A., *Airpower in Peripheral Conflict: The French Experience in Africa*, Santa Monica, Calif.: RAND, R-3660-AF, 1989.

Machina, Mark, "Choice Under Uncertainty: Problems Solved and Unsolved," *Economic Perspectives*, Summer 1987, pp. 121–154.

Mako, W., *U.S. Ground Forces and the Defense of Central Europe*, Washington, D.C.: Brookings Institution, 1983.

Mandelbaum, M., *The Nuclear Question*, New York: Cambridge University Press, 1979.

Maoz, Z., "Resolve, Capabilities, and the Outcomes of Interstate Disputes," *Journal of Conflict Resolution*, Vol. 27, No. 2, 1983, pp. 195–230.

March, James, and Herbert Simon, *Organizations*, New York: Wiley, 1958.

Maxon, Y., *Control of Japanese Foreign Policy: A Study of Civil-Military Rivalry, 1930–1945*, Berkeley: University of California Press, 1957.

Mearsheimer, J., *Conventional Deterrence*, Ithaca, N.Y.:   Cornell University Press, 1983.

Moraes, F., *Jawaharlal Nehru: A Biography*, New York: Macmillan, 1956.

Morgan, Patrick, *Deterrence: A Conceptual Analysis*, 2nd ed., Beverly Hills, Calif.: Sage Publications, 1983, Ch. 2.

Morton, L., "The Japanese Decision for War," *U.S. Naval Institute Proceedings*, Vol. 80, December 1954, pp. 1325–1337.

Mylroie, L., "Why Saddam Hussein Invaded Kuwait," *Orbis*, Vol. 37, No. 1, Winter 1993.

Organski, A., *The Stages of Political Development*, New York: Knopf, 1965.

Pape, R. A., "Coercion and Military Strategy: Why Denial Works and Punishment Doesn't," *Journal of Strategic Studies*, Vol. 15, No. 4, December 1992, pp. 423–475.

Quandt, W., *Decade of Decision: American Policy Toward the Arab-Israeli Conflict, 1967–1976*, Berkeley: University of California Press, 1977.

Quattrone, George, and Amos Tversky, "Contracting Rational and Psychological Analyses of Political Choice," *American Political Science Review*, Vol. 82, No. 3, September 1988.

Riad, M., *The Struggle for Peace in the Middle East*, London: Quartet Books, 1981.

Rustow, D., *A World of Nations: Problems of Political Modernization*, Washington, D.C.: Brookings Institution, 1967.

Sadat, Anwar, *In Search of Identity: An Autobiography*, New York: Harper & Row, 1977.

Safran, N., *Israel: The Embattled Ally*, Cambridge: Harvard University Press, 1981.

Sagan, S., "The Origins of the Pacific War," *Journal of Interdisciplinary History*, Spring 1988.

Schelling, Thomas, *The Strategy of Conflict*, New York: Oxford University Press, 1963.

Schwartz, D., *NATO's Nuclear Dilemmas*, Washington, D.C.: Brookings Institution, 1983.

Schwarz, Benjamin, *Casualties, Public Opinion, and U.S. Military Intervention: Implications for U.S. Regional Deterrence Strategies*, Santa Monica, Calif.: RAND, MR-431-A/AF, 1994.

Shimshoni, Jonathan, *Israel and Conventional Deterrence: Border Warfare from 1953 to 1970*, Ithaca: Cornell University Press, 1988.

Simon, Herbert, "A Behavioral Model of Rational Choice," *Quarterly Journal of Economics*, Vol. 69, February 1955.

Snyder, Glenn, *Deterrence and Defense*, Princeton University Press, 1961.

Stein, Janice Gross, "Deterrence and Compellence in the Gulf, 1990–91: A Failed or Impossible Task?" *International Security*, Vol. 17, No. 2, Fall, 1992, pp. 147–179.

Stein, Janice, "The Arab-Israeli War of 1967: Inadvertent War Through Miscalculated Escalation," in A. George, ed., *Avoiding*

War: Problems of Crisis Management, Boulder, Colo.: Westview Press, 1991, pp. 126–159.

Stein, Janice, "Extended Deterrence in the Middle East: American Strategy Reconsidered," *World Politics*, Vol. 39. No. 3, 1987, pp. 326–352.

Togo, S., *The Cause of Japan*, New York: Simon and Schuster, 1956.

Toland, J., *The Rising Sun*, New York: Random House, 1970.

Ulam, A., *Expansion and Coexistence*, 2nd ed., New York: Praeger Press, 1974.

Wanandi, Jusuf, "The International Implications of Third-World Conflict: A Third World Perspective," *Third World Conflict and International Security, Part 1*, Adelphi Papers, No. 161, London: IISS, 1981.

Whiting, A., *China Crosses the Yalu: The Decision to Enter the Korean War*, Stanford, Calif.: Stanford University Press, 1960.

Whiting, A., *The Chinese Calculus of Deterrence: India and Indochina*, Ann Arbor: University of Michigan Press, 1975.

Wilkening, Dean, and Kenneth Watman, *Nuclear Deterrence in a Regional Context*, Santa Monica, Calif.: RAND, MR-500-A/AF, 1994.

Wiseman, H., *Political Systems: Some Sociological Approaches*, London: Routledge & Kegan Paul, 1966.

Wohlstetter, R., *Pearl Harbor: Warning and Decision*, Stanford, Calif.: Stanford University Press, 1962.

Wolf, Barry, *When the Weak Attack the Strong: Failures of Deterrence*, Santa Monica, Calif.: RAND, N-3261-A, 1991.

Zagare, Frank, "Rationality and Deterrence," *World Politics*, January 1990, pp. 238–260.